3/97  LR/LEND/001

UNIVERSITY OF
WOLVERHAMPTON

D1460560

WITHDRAWN

WP 2206652 7

Living in
LONDON

KAREN HOWES

Photographs by
SIMON UPTON

Preface by
TERENCE CONRAN

UNIVERSITY OF WOLVERHAMPTON
LEARNING RESOURCES

Acc No.
2206652

CLASS
720,
9421
HOW

CONTROL
20 8 0136615

DATE
-6. JUN 2000

SITE
W

Flammarion

To all those, residents and visitors alike,
who enrich London with their individuality,
enthusiasm and eccentricity.

Artistic Director Marc Walter – Bela Vista
Editorial Director Ghislaine Bavoillot
Editorial Management Orhan Memed
Colour separation by Colourscan France
Production Murielle Vaux

Flammarion
26, rue Racine
75006 Paris

original title *L'Art de Vivre à Londres*

© 1999 Flammarion All rights reserved.
No part of this publication may be reproduced in any form or by any
means written, electronic, information retrieval system, or photocopy
without permission from Flammarion.

ISBN 2-08013-661-5
Numéro d'édition: FA 3661

Printed and bound in Italy by G. Canale & Co. SpA, Borgaro
Dépôt légal: January 1999

CONTENTS

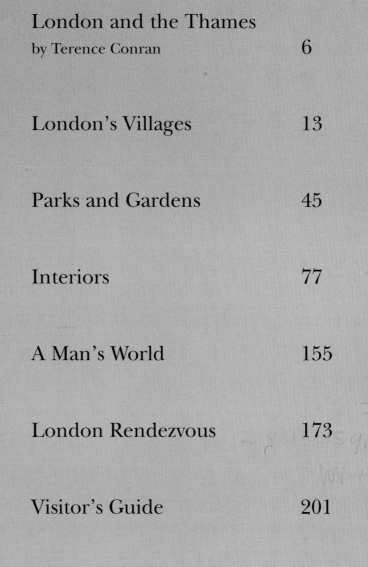

London and the Thames
by Terence Conran

St Katharine's Dock, opened in 1828, was built on an area conveniently located near the City between London Docks and Tower Bridge. The dock facilitated the unloading of wool, sugar and rubber and communities of dockers and sailors made their homes nearby. Since its demise in 1968, St Katherine's Dock has become a yachting marina, the warehouses and wharves replaced with smart apartment blocks and restaurants for well-heeled City workers and tourists alike. Small craft and the occasional larger vessel still come and go through the narrow lock, jostling for a mooring alongside the houseboats of more permanent residents.

I have lived in London all my adult life, and yet the city continues to surprise me. No one—not even the cab drivers with their encyclopaedic knowledge of London streets—can honestly claim to know every road and every building, to have noted and appreciated every architectural detail or new shop or restaurant. One of London's greatest assets is that there are always secrets waiting to be discovered. The city combines history and tradition with energy and flux; it is reassuringly familiar at the same time as being a constant source of innovation and inspiration.

As everyone will tell you—and as this book beautifully illustrates—London is a city of villages, each with its very distinct characteristics. The people who live in these villages behave often as if they belong to a tribe in the vigorous defense of their own patch. Londoners who might think nothing of complaining about the city in general, display a tremendous sense of pride for their own part of town. People who live in Islington are convinced of its superiority over Camden Town, and vice versa; but both are united by a collective aversion to crossing the river into south London. (At least, until we started opening restaurants there!)

I love moving between different parts of the city, marvelling at how areas so close to one

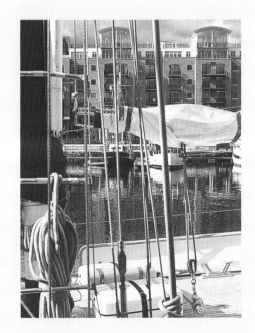

another can be so different. The grimy chic and frenetic energy of Soho cannot be more than a ten-minute walk from the elegance and the almost patronising grandeur of St James's with its gentlemen's tailors and its gentlemen's clubs, its auction houses and galleries. Many of the people who live in Soho are every bit as affluent as residents of St James's—it is just that they choose to display their status in an utterly different way.

One of the things for which London has rightly been famous over the last 30 years or more is its street fashion. Paris gave the world *haute couture*, London gave it Mods and Punks and New Romantics and a panoply of other do-it-your-self looks. Fashion goes from street to catwalk rather than the other way around. And that, when you consider it, is quite odd. The British are often characterised as rather staid and conservative, quiet and conventional, yet in London more than almost anywhere else in the world, there is one simple rule: anything goes.

The different personalities of London's villages make it impossible to come up with a definitive picture of London. A day spent by the river in Hammersmith would be very different from one browsing around Brick Lane market and then exploring the City, which in turn would have little in common with an afternoon spent wandering between cafés and bars and specialist shops in Soho. London is a city of almost infinite variety, and Londoners are adept at fine-tuning their

The warehouses which make up Butler's Wharf on the south bank of the Thames were once used to store the chests of tea, coffee and spices unloaded from boats which sailed up to Tower Bridge. In the 1980s, these Victorian buildings were salvaged by Sir Terence Conran from the dereliction and decay into which they had fallen. Butler's Wharf now comprises apartments, offices, several Conran restaurants and a selection of shops.

characters and their wardrobes to each particular environment.

Living in London can be a very expensive business, yet for many people the advantages far outweigh the disadvantages. The sheer wealth of experiences that the capital can offer seems to increase by the day, and in the last 40 or 50 years the pace of change has been extraordinary. In the 1950s, when I was starting up as a young furniture-maker, I would quite often find myself walking home at night through the leafy streets around Regent's Park. Some of the houses would still have their shutters open, which gave anyone who was nosy or interested—like me—a chance to look into the brightly lit living-rooms. Most of them were fairly uniform, but every so often I would spot somewhere that looked a bit different and think, "I bet the people who live there are interesting." These days, I am sure, there would be many more of these glimpsed interiors that would prompt such a response.

More than any other European city, London has been at the vanguard in the conversion of disused factories, warehouses, schools and churches, even 1960s office blocks, for domestic use. This trend has led people to rediscover parts of London, injecting it with new life. Clerkenwell (on the fringes of the City to the east) has in the last five years become a hotspot of galleries, bars and interesting shops and restaurants, as architects, designers and entrepreneurs have bought up abandoned buildings and converted them to loft-style apartments.

I have some first-hand experience in this process, having been involved in the regeneration of Butler's Wharf on the south bank of the Thames. Today it is an increasingly popular part of London in which to live, work and socialise. There are four restaurants and two bars along the riverfront, as well as the Design Museum. The area boasts a lively mix of other restaurants, shops,

Butler's Wharf has been thoughtfully converted with much of the Victorian detailing incorporated into the new design. This spectacular penthouse which overlooks Tower Bridge benefits from a three-storey conservatory and is all the more striking due to the imaginative use of white clapboard on the exterior.

galleries and warehouse conversions. It is also just across the river from the City which affords fantastic views of two of London's most famous landmarks: the Tower of London and Tower Bridge. For me, it has so many advantages that I moved my offices here and built an apartment at the top of the building.

Butler's Wharf today is very different from the place I first saw in the mid-1980s. I was at an office party on a pleasure-boat going down the Thames, and as we passed underneath Tower Bridge I saw on the south bank a fantastic collection of Victorian warehouses. In the 19th century, these had been used to store deliveries of tea, coffee and spices from around the world and the surrounding area had been a thriving part of the city. Alas, containerisation put pay to the shipping industry, and after the Second World War, the area went into decline. Artists of a distinctly Bohemian nature made a stab at using the vast warehouses as studio-squats, but even they eventually ceded tenancy to the growing population of rats. Butler's Wharf became a 12-acre site that was completely and utterly derelict.

I was convinced that Butler's Wharf had the potential to become one of the most vibrant parts of London. Conventional wisdom said that money would never cross the river (there's a lot of snobbery associated with the supposedly miserable shortcomings of South London), but I firmly believed that Butler's Wharf would be able to support the kind of regeneration that had turned Covent Garden from a disused fruit and vegetable market into one of the most popular areas of London. To my mind, in fact, Covent Garden has become a victim of its own success and the area around the market serves to attract tourists rather than to provide for the needs of the local community.

When I formed a consortium of people to redevelop Butler's Wharf, we won permission for a mixed-use scheme of apartments, offices, shops, restaurants and the Design Museum, among other elements. Almost as soon as we began work, the enormity of the task became apparent: whilst we had budgeted for the

The tall windows in the brick façade of the former Victorian warehouse at Butler's Wharf allow one to gaze out benevolently over the Thames. An original chimney and gable have been incorporated into a rooftop conservatory which runs the width of the conversion.

A view down-river from the South Bank Centre on the left bank towards Blackfriars Bridge. The domed roof of St Paul's Cathedral, Christopher Wren's masterpiece, distinguishes itself from the skyscrapers that now crowd the City skyline.

almost total lack of utilities and infrastructure, we had not counted on the main riverfront warehouse having inadequate foundations. This was a costly problem we had to remedy before we could even start on renovation.

It is at once remarkable to consider what has been achieved and to imagine how much will change. The Thames—alas one of London's most neglected assets—will soon have more things of cultural significance along its south bank than it does on its north. People will be able to walk east along the Thames from the spruced-up South Bank Centre (home to the National Theatre, National Film Theatre, Festival Hall, Hayward Galley and Museum of the Moving Image) to the Tate Museum of Modern Art at Bankside, thence to the Globe Theatre and on to the Design Museum. With the Millennium celebrations at Greenwich and the resulting increase in river traffic, my hope is that when people think of London, their mental map will have shifted eastwards ever so slightly.

One of the thrills of living in London is the city's ability to reveal something new and exciting at every opportunity. This happens because the people who live here—not just the "born and bred" Londoners, but those who make the city their adopted home—are attracted by its vitality, diversity and energy. No one can predict what the next big trend will be—who knows, it might be a reaction against the youth culture that has seen London in the Nineties being compared to the "swinging Sixties". London's strength lies in its ability to combine the old and the new, adapting traditions rather than throwing them out, bulldozing them down or outlawing them. Less bourgeois and friendlier than Paris, more civilised than New York, greener than Tokyo and more human than Los Angeles, London seems to me to be the city that best combines what is good and exciting about city living. I love travelling the world and visiting new places, but I am always pleased to come home and discover another area of London that I have never seen before.

Sailing boats of all shapes and sizes are moored alongside the wooden walkways which run around the perimeter of St Katharine's Dock. Their riggings slap joyously in the wind, mingling with the mad cries of the seagulls that circle overhead.

Terence Conran

LONDON'S VILLAGES

While residents reflect on the fading memory of a tranquil weekend, roads fill up with Monday's early morning rush hour, underground stations teem with commuters and overland trains shuttle thousands more into the City, swelling the ranks of daytime Londoners to capacity. Apart from its obvious economic importance, this daily surge is vital to the ever changing mood of London, bringing with it renewed enthusiasm and fresh ideas, as well as new demands on the city and its residents.

To avoid stagnation, cities need such constant flux and reflux, and one of the elements which keeps London so popular with residents and visitors alike is that it never stands still. This zest for change—and London's uncanny ability to re-invent itself—has proved to be a lasting attraction for the waves of immigrant populations who have settled here over the years. Bringing with them new styles, tastes and expectations, these adopted Londoners add a striking character to their new environment, their interpretation of the city's architectural heritage bearing a direct influence on its future.

London's appearance today—the layout of its streets and squares, terraces and gardens—is a legacy of this mix of English and European styles from the eighteenth and nineteenth centuries. Although earlier architectural influences still exist, these have, for the most part, been incorporated into a visionary Victorian master plan, which, up to the present, has managed to resist successive attempts to change the overall look of central London.

The variety of architecture for which London is justifiably famous ranges from the Victorian red brick houses and apartments of Lennox Gardens in Chelsea (preceding double page) to the grand terraces of Cadogan Place in Belgravia (left) with their elegant façades of white stucco and imposing columned entrances.

Each neighbourhood has its flavour. In Notting Hill a contemporary interpretation of Victorian elegance produces a colourful terrace of houses repeated in shades of yellow and blue.

The influence of the Georgian period—with its idiosyncratic narrow brick houses built over several storeys, their tall sash windows and ornate fanlights posed above solid wooden doors—can be found throughout London. From the cobbled streets of Spitalfields and the squares of Islington, along the elegant terraces of Hampstead and Richmond, to the elaborate mansions overlooking the Thames on Chelsea Embankment, the grace and charm of these many architectural styles have endured to the present day.

The Victorians, however, did not much like Georgian London and with their era came a dramatic change in architectural design. They created terraces of grand houses with façades of white stucco and columned entrances, influenced by the Italianate style of the day—a look now forever synonymous with most of central

London. As building pushed ever westward from the City, rows of stucco terraces formed the new residential areas in Knightsbridge and South Kensington. Daring property developers went as far as Notting Hill with their grandiose schemes and designed streets of stucco villas and mansions in the vastness of the wasteland they found there.

The grandeur and generous proportions of these houses, however, were replaced in the 1880s by a new style of inner-city construction: mansion block dwellings. Overcrowding, lack of space, and the beginnings of a new social awareness had persuaded Victorians to turn towards such subdivided housing. Blocks of flats were built of red brick, rather than the more fragile stone and stucco, and were destined for a somewhat less affluent population. The work of architect of the day, Norman Shaw—who was supposedly influenced by his visits to Paris—these were not the style of flats that Londoners are accustomed to live in today. Victorians still needed accommodation for their servants, a socially acceptable number of rooms for themselves and, most important of all, a good location overlooking a park or garden. For those without the means to afford a flat in London, the only solution was to move from the centre to the villages on the periphery of the city. Here, land was cheaper and ownership of individual houses still a possibility. Thus, London slowly began to spread, engulfing open land and provincial villages to accommodate its rapidly increasing population. As new bridges were built across the Thames, residences south of the river were also considered, and

Victorian elegance reached out as far as Clapham. Eventually, at the turn of the twentieth century, even further flung towns, such as Putney and Richmond, were absorbed into greater London.

In the Edwardian period, the emerging middle class moved into nondescript streets of identical, red-brick houses built in wholesale fashion, each with a pocket handkerchief for a garden, spilling out into much of the west and south of London, filling in the gaps from Clapham and Wandsworth to Battersea and Fulham.

When London was rebuilt after the ravages of Second World War, and as space had become noticeably short on the ground, restoration was to include some of the city's first tower blocks.

London seems always to have been a crowded city but, until the property boom

The red brick façades of many of the Victorian squares in central London are often embellished with stone or stucco for additional decorative effect. Windows and doors may be highlighted as in this detail of the façade at Eleven Cadogan Gardens, a charming private hotel in Chelsea (far left). Entrances to buildings are made more important by incorporating stucco into the design (below) and even by the addition of balconies and terraces supported by elegant columns as shown on the façade of this mansion block in Cadogan Square (right).

of the 1960s, it was never really considered to be a tall one. The Victorian vistas planned so carefully are now interrupted or impeded by the thoughtless positioning of overwhelming tower blocks. Streets of Victorian elegance are overshadowed by the tiers of concrete council flats, built to replace much of the city's former slum dwellings, the grey façades of these de-

characteristic pulleys, heavy iron beams and interior brick walls associated with their former trade. A leading influence in this regeneration was Sir Terence Conran, whose project at Butler's Wharf included residential accommodation, shops and restaurants. The rejuvenation of the Docklands heralded a new period of growth in the property market and along

For an erstwhile seafaring nation, the Thames plays a relatively unimportant part in the lives of most Londoners. Unused as a thoroughfare except by the occasional barge or pleasure boat, it is spanned by several bridges, one of the more beautiful being Albert Bridge, which links Chelsea with Battersea. Its elegant silhouette is picked out at night by hundreds of tiny lights which cast a soft glow onto the blackness of the river below.

pressing buildings emphasised in their ugliness by the dark patches of damp and grime left by a combination of harsh weather and urban pollution.

By the 1980s, the constant search for a building site in a city where there was little space left to develop, prompted a fresh look at the wasteland of derelict factories and riverside wharves and warehouses. Neglected since the barges and commercial freighters had ceased to ply their trade as far up-river as Tower Bridge, many of these imposing Victorian bastions have been thoughtfully converted, retaining the

with it a resurgence of interest in the Thames itself. Having been virtually ignored by London residents for so many years, the river acquired a new and important significance which continues unabated.

Glass replaced brick as the banks of the Thames continued to change. The huge development at Canary Wharf, which, through London's recent recession, struggled to justify its existence so far down-river, ironically helped mark the end of London's newspaper mecca in Fleet Street, when the media giants decamped to the wharf *en*

A marina at St Katharine's Dock near Tower Bridge is the luxurious setting for private sailing boats (above) which enter the river through a narrow lock as did the merchant ships at the height of the British Empire.

masse. Its tall glass tower stands sentinel at the east end of the city—a symbol of endurance certainly, and perhaps a sign of future architectural influence.

In the mean time, up-river, Chelsea Wharf, another glass and concrete complex in West London with its own hotels, shops and restaurants, was luring the new wealthy young business executive to a self-imposed, luxury exile, complete with security guards and camera surveillance. A far cry from the accepted lifestyle of the traditional Londoner, this trend in self-contained communities secured behind high walls and electric gates seems to reflect the new paranoia of the 1990s. Other architects, such as Sir Norman Foster, have taken advantage of the river to design buildings of little except glass, the vast expanse of windows reflecting every nuance and change in the mood of the Thames.

On the south bank of the Thames the twenty-first century meets the nineteenth as a metal pedestrian walkway joins the restored Victorian warehouses of New Concordia Wharf in Bermondsey (left).

A community of brightly coloured houseboats jostles for position on the incoming tide at one of Chelsea's smartest moorings, overlooked by the imposing Georgian mansions along Cheyne Walk in Chelsea (above).

An apartment at Riverside One, on the south bank of the river between Battersea Bridge and Albert Bridge, takes advantage of its splendid location, the vast expanse of its floor to ceiling windows reflecting every nuance and change in the mood of the Thames. Designed by Sir Norman Foster, the space is filled with light, even on the gloomiest of days. The uniform white interior, created by minimalist Claudio Silvestrin plays with this intense light. Frosted glass panels offer privacy, should one ever want to shut out the spectacular view over Chelsea.

Traditional London architecture is illustrated by these two street scenes: a shop in Little Venice with its Victorian street lamp (below, left) and a typical corner cafe on the Upper Mall in Chiswick (below, right).

London is a city full of change, growing and adapting itself as circumstances dictate. Its vast scale and superficial anonymity belie an intimacy unlike that of any other great city. Full of surprises and amazing characters, London is a melting pot of separate villages, each contributing to the city a unique flavour and style, accumulated and perfected over the centuries. Ask someone if they come from London and the answer will probably be, no, they come from Hampstead, or Chelsea, or the East End.

A village identity carries with it a sense of being, and most people who live in London instinctively recognise their immediate neighbourhood, gravitating to that bit of the city they know best, then visiting the

rest with the reluctance and insecurity of strangers. Restaurants, cinemas, and all sorts of shops—from news-stands to bookshops to clothing boutiques—are located just outside one's door. It is this village identity that provides colour and variety, contributing to an identity that causes so many people of a variety of nationalities

as examples of the diversity to be found within London. Inevitably, these are the villages at the centre of the city, those of historical interest and architectural beauty.

The City is the oldest part of London, its heart, but with no few open spaces, it could be easily mistaken for the newest development. As Europe's financial capital, it

A tranquil moment in the life of the Thames, the spindly legs of an old jetty, revealed by the ebbing tide, interrupt the view from the South Bank across to the City and the distant dome of St Paul's Cathedral.

and cultures to adopt different parts of London for themselves.

Each of the twenty or more villages of London, sub-divided nowadays into over thirty boroughs, reflects its historical origins and past traditions in the influences which in turn bear a direct relation to the the appearance of the city today.

Instead of describing each individual village, some of the more interesting and universally recognised have been selected

has benefited from a great deal of investment, resulting in a concentrated display of skyscrapers, new office buildings, rebuilt roads and redesigned train stations. With the last vestige of character eliminated from its streets, the City could be any financial centre in the world. Yet, only a stone's throw away, dwarfed by these same glass towers and dazzled by the sunlight reflected off their façades, is a village which could be found nowhere else but in London.

SPITALFIELDS AND CLERKENWELL

The narrow, cobbled streets of Georgian townhouses lead off at a tangent from one of London's busiest arteries in the East End. Huge juggernauts join lines of stationary vehicles queuing to enter the City. The throb of combustion engines reverberates against the neighbouring buildings, a threatening contemporary intrusion into this small area where time appears to have stood still. In the sixteenth century, Spitalfields Market was a field of grass and Brick Lane a deep and rutted track used by carts for transporting bricks from the kilns into Whitechapel. Open fields soon gave way to tenement houses and·by 1729 Hawksmoor's beautiful Christ Church Spitalfields was to change the skyline forever.

Spitalfields has always been known for its non-conformity and individuality. Over the centuries, immigrants were attracted to the area and French weavers, who had made a home for themselves there in the seventeenth century, were soon joined by Huguenot refugees. They set up a flourishing silk-weaving business which consolidated the area's reputation in the eighteenth century. So successful were they that the master weavers and silk merchants built beautiful Georgian houses in Fournier and Elder Streets. Many of these buildings still stand today, recalling an early prosperity, having ironically been saved from demolition by economic decline.

At the start of the nineteenth century, poverty was widespread and the village was completely overwhelmed by its housing inadequacies. The resulting slums were later torn down to make way for the roads on which today's traffic piles up in angry frustration, and the rebuilding of the area commenced in earnest. The silk weavers' workshops were replaced by those of furriers and clothiers, and the market was extended, at the cost of a number of surrounding Georgian buildings.

Spitalfields Market continued to be the centre of attraction, selling fruit and vegetables until 1991. Residents who moved into the area some thirty years ago, recall an eccentricity, a gathering of free-spirited people, where individualism was encouraged and conformity decried. Houses, with no heating or running water, were occupied by people looking for the meaning of life, adventurers in search of an identity and sure of finding it amidst the history of Hawksmoor's Spitalfields.

Today, the clothing workshops have been taken over by the latest wave of immigrants, the Bangladeshi, who carry on the

Author Peter Ackroyd (below) has set several of his novels, including *Hawksmoor* and *The House of Dr. Dee,* in the grim surroundings of Clerkenwell and Spitalfields of times gone by. Ackroyd is especially well-known for *Dickens,* a superb biography revealing his combined talents of scholar and novelist. The writer's fascination with the city has now involved him in another major project, *The Biography of London.*

History seems to seep out of the very brickwork of many of the Georgian houses along Elder and Fournier Streets in the heart of Spitalfields. Crooked doors open straight onto the cobbled street, while closed shutters protect the darkened interiors from the inquisitive eyes of passers-by (far left and right).

tradition of rag traders in Brick Lane. Petticoat Lane market continues to thrive on the fringes of the City, while the flower market, early on a Sunday morning, brings welcome colour to Columbia Road.

The East End has now become the preferred home of London's artistically inclined. With the relocation of the fruit and vegetable market and the closure of several factories, Spitalfields has managed to lure a succession of artists and sculptors. Attracted initially by the rows of vacant brick buildings in suitably dilapidated streets, where rents were cheap and space put no limit on experimentation, artists have installed themselves, far from the traditional Bohemian centres in Chelsea and Notting Hill. Galleries and exhibition spaces in neighbouring Clerkenwell have sprung up, and as attention is focused on artistic novelty and achievement, the area attracts new would-be residents.

Clerkenwell is the most recent of London's forlorn and abandoned villages to experience a resurrection. Decayed and semi-derelict buildings have been instilled with new life, others have been demolished only to have new ones put up in their place. Loft living has come to Clerkenwell and with it the music and media industries have taken up residence, trendy restaurants mushroom, with designer shops and more art galleries sure to follow.

North and slightly uphill from Smithfield, Clerkenwell was always considered to be outside the City of London. As a result of this geographical limitation, it became

An unexpected hint of colour and frivolity in the window of a hat shop at the entrance to the former site of Spitalfields Market (above) counterbalances the occasional glimpse through a small window into an unlit interior, and the dark brick and black shutters of No. Eleven and Half Fournier Street (right and far right).

popular with foreign refugees who, discouraged by higher rates and restrictive guild practices, settled beyond the City limits. Clerkenwell thus became the centre for clock and watch-makers, jewellers, printers and cabinet makers. Together with contemporary furniture designers, these artisans have returned to the area in the last decade.

Watered by abundant springs and the Fleet River, Clerkenwell was also a fashionable spa town, following the discovery of wells in the garden of Thomas Sadler's music house, birthplace of the Sadler's Wells School of Ballet.

Social decline eventually led to the deterioration of entire streets of splendid houses into areas of slums. Although Clerkenwell retains its identity, it was merged with Islington in 1965.

Only a few of London's residents can enjoy the Regent's Canal from the seclusion of their own back gardens, as in Islington (above). Others work on the water or make their homes in the many houseboats and barges which are moored along this stretch, appropriately named Little Venice (left).

ISLINGTON

Perched on a hill-top, Islington was appreciated and patronised by successive monarchs and noted for its imposing mansions. In the eighteenth century, with a reputation for quality dairy farms and fresh spring water, it shared neighbouring Clerkenwell's popularity as a recreational retreat.

Its good fortunes came and went. Academies and nursery gardens were followed in the nineteenth century by brick

A view through the trees over the tranquil, communal garden of Lonsdale Square in Islington, where residents can enjoy a lazy afternoon in the sun amidst roses and herbaceous borders.

fields that catered to London's building boom. These in turn were built upon to provide housing for Islington's booming population, as the Regent's Canal (completed in 1820) and the railways brought more well-to-do city workers to the suburbs.

Islington's prosperity went into decline as the century drew to a close. A poorer working-class gradually took over the once elegant Georgian squares and terraces, Canonbury and Barnsbury alone retaining a certain gentility. The writer, Evelyn Waugh, who lived in Canonbury Square in 1928, summed up the area as "a shabby genteel square, no longer a fashionable quarter but agreeably symmetrical and soothing to the eye."

Subject to constant change and regeneration, Islington once again became fashionable in the early 1960s with the arrival of architects and media professionals. This rekindling of interest brought with it investment and a degree of prosperity. The number of shops and restaurants increased, small theatres introduced a Bohemian element (many of them today still run as public house theatres) and, in 1964, an antiques market was started in Camden Passage.

Since then, Islington has enjoyed the return of its former fashionable reputation, with the terraces of Georgian houses struggling to regain the grandeur and presence of bygone days.

It seems, however, to be just this slightly down-at-heel appearance which appeals to many of Islington's new wave of residents, who prefer the more low-key demands of this village to the smarter pretensions of Chelsea or Hampstead. Yet, once again, what began as a Bohemian movement has ended up at a point where only the well-to-do can afford to live in certain neighbourhoods of this village.

Compounding this success, Camden Passage has achieved an international reputation in the antiques trade, with many important dealers taking up residence and opening shops there. Its Saturday antiques market is a rival to that of Portobello Road in Notting Hill, while nearby Chapel Market, now trading for well over one hundred years, remains one of London's most famous street markets.

HAMPSTEAD

North-west of Islington, Hampstead and Highgate stand on two hills overlooking London. Although the two villages are geographically close, their histories differ. Highgate was much the smaller, and due to its steep hill, less accessible from London. It remains an elegant village today, retaining its own identity with many of the stately old houses still standing.

Hampstead's good fortunes began with the commercial development of its mineral springs in the early eighteenth century, when water was collected from Hampstead Wells and brought daily to the old Flask Tavern (this site is now occupied by its Victorian replacement), where it was bottled and taken to London. To encourage people from London to come to Hampstead and take the waters, an Assembly Room was built on what came to be known as Well Walk. The Pump Room was dressed up with a concert hall and ballroom, while lodgings were made available in various taverns. As demand soon outstripped availability, small cottages were hastily built and streets of larger houses designed. Tea houses and souvenir shops were quick to catch on.

Most of the construction of Hampstead at this time took place on the slopes of Hampstead Hill. Considered too hilly for farming, clusters of small Georgian cottages still cling like limpets to the steep gradients of the streets, while sets of crooked steps descend to join pathways and alleys far below them. As Daniel Defoe said of Hampstead in 1724, "'Tis so near to

Heaven, that I dare not say it can be a proper situation for any but a race of mountaineers." At Frognal, in the heart of the village, a number of imposing mansions had already been built in Defoe's time. These homes of successful merchants are proof of the village's wealth; the majority were built on generous plots of land surrounded by high walls.

Church Row must be the finest surviving example of this period in Hampstead's architectural history. Nearly all the houses on either side of this short street date from the early eighteenth century. Some were occupied at the time as permanent residences, others used as holiday homes. The street, like Well Walk, was planted with lime trees and became a fashionable promenade. The Church of St John at the end of the Row was built between 1745 and 1747 on the site of an old chapel. Its steep cemetery, which continues on the opposite side of the road, holds the remains of John Constable and many other famous former residents.

The Flask, a Victorian pub built on the site of the original eighteenth-century tavern on Flask Walk, in the heart of Hampstead Village, provides a quiet corner in which to enjoy a pint over a newspaper.

In Islington, an industrious antique dealer polishes a chandelier in the doorway of his shop in Camden Passage, where an antique market to rival Portobello Road takes place every Saturday.

Church Row (left and top right) is regarded today as one of the finest surviving terraces of early eighteenth-century townhouses in England. The detailing on each of the houses distinguishes it from its immediate neighbour, and many of the buildings are set back from the wide pavement of York stone behind black iron railings.

Following the social and economic trends experienced by other villages on the outskirts of London, Hampstead's success as a spa was short-lived. It was situated too close to the city to remain exclusive for long, and its demise started with the arrival of day-trippers of the wrong social calibre and without the requisite money to burn.

Hampstead has, however, always remained an exclusive place to live and, since the eighteenth century, has been the favourite rendezvous of many literary and artistic figures, drawn to the area for its country air and pastoral scenery. Over the years, these have included artists such as George Romney, William Holman Hunt, John Constable, Joshua Reynolds and Thomas Gainsborough, along with writers and poets including George du Maurier, John Galsworthy, Anthony Trollope, D.H. Lawrence, J.B. Priestley, and John Keats, whose house is now a museum.

By the end of the nineteenth century, prosperous Victorians had staked their claim, building larger and yet more imposing villas and mansions along Haverstock Hill, while stuccoed Regency villas and terraces were concentrated around Downshire Hill. The mansions were of short-term appeal to the clutch of Victorian artists that frequented Hampstead. The sheer size of these over-indulgent buildings made many impractical to live in and they have since been turned into schools and privately-run hotels.

Although it has now been absorbed by London, and its main street is full of shops identical to anywhere else in the city, Hampstead's appeal and exclusivity

Elsewhere in Hampstead, narrow streets of cottages cling to the steep hillside and small, flagged courtyards provide a sheltered oasis for plants and terracotta pots of flowers (below).

continue to this day. The collection of wonderful buildings, together with the village's heightened sense of its own history, set it apart from other all others.

NOTTING HILL

In contrast, the village of Notting Hill was a late developer. Until well into the nine-

It is a bright Saturday morning on the Portobello Road in Notting Hill, where the milling throngs of tourists and local enthusiasts wander past shops and stalls of antiques in search of a bargain.

teenth century, the Ladbroke Estate, which forms the greater part of this village, was completely rural, its income generated as late as the 1850s from brick-making, potteries and piggeries.

In the 1830s, James Weller Ladbroke, the local landowner, together with architect Thomas Allason, devised the layout for Ladbroke Grove, on which were built large detached and semi-detached houses destined for wealthy residents. Allason was inspired by John Nash's work in Regent's Park (which took from 1812 to 1828 to complete) but, in Ladbroke's eagerness, houses went up faster than occupants for them could be found and freeholds were sold cheaply as investments. Those located

near the potteries, which were essentially no better than slums, did not sell at all. With the financial crash in 1825, Allason's plans were never completed. Whole streets remained half built and empty for long periods and Ladbroke Gardens was still unfinished as late as 1870, earning it the name "Coffin Row." Despite the interludes, crises and delays, the Ladbroke Estate slowly came together, a vision of elegant stucco houses in garden settings, with squares and crescents of terraces overlooking communal gardens, their grandeur taking advantage of the hilly terrain.

The pattern of boom and bust was to continue here as elsewhere in London. Notting Hill, as it looks today, is the result of extensive redevelopment in the 1950s, which saw the wholesale demolition of the remaining slums and streets of shabby houses.

The construction in the 1960s of contemporary Notting Hill's great geographical divide, the M40 Westway (London's elevated section of motorway), provided a psychological barrier between rich and poor, as West Indians from London's East End moved into the terraces north of this demarcation line. In retrospect, the arrival of a multi-ethnic society was to be the making of Notting Hill, creating a village of colour and cultural variety. Not always harmonious, Notting Hill has grown in stature and awareness over the years and is currently enjoying a financial and social resurgence.

Sixty years ago, Portobello Road was just another of London's numerous street markets, lined with rows of shabby shops,

which took advantage of the passing trade around the colourful fruit and vegetable stalls. A few barrows selling antiques and junk would appear on a Saturday morning. Now that London has become a centre of the antique trade, the Portobello Road has developed from a simple neighbourhood market to one of international reputation. Today, the old provision stalls are overshadowed by the antique market and the shops that line the street.

Westbourne Grove, once labelled Bankrupt Avenue, together with Ledbury Road, is now at the hub of Notting Hill's current boom. Expensive delicatessens, street cafes and glorious flower shops spill onto the pavement. Antique dealers, interior designers, shops full of fashion accessories and textiles, art galleries and boutiques jostle for custom, all maximising on the new "in" trend of this small area. Bars and restaurants reflect the multi-cultural appeal which has attracted so many new residents to Notting Hill. At the same time, terraces of sadly neglected Victorian houses north of the M40 divide are now undergoing gentrification, the prices pushing former residents further north and west. Their places are being taken by designers and stylists, photographers and fashion gurus and the best of today's movers and shakers. Living beyond the M40 has lost its social stigma. Notting Hill has finally arrived.

T he bright display of assorted blooms in metal buckets has made the Turquoise Isle (where florists Wild at Heart have set up shop) a local landmark, while the daily business of selling fruit and vegetables carries on from barrows laden with colourful produce to catch the eye of the casual passer-by (below).

C rescents and streets of imposing stucco-fronted houses and terraces lead off Ladbroke Grove, the main artery into Notting Hill. When the wisteria comes into flower in late Spring, this house will be completely hidden behind a pale mauve screen (above).

KENSINGTON

At the beginning of the eighteenth century, Kensington was a small village, clustered around its church, barely three miles from London. Its popularity and fashionable status grew not only from the presence of the court at Kensington Palace, but also from its reputation as a healthy location, best known for the Brompton Park Nursery—over one hundred acres of nursery gardens which stretched as far as Earl's Court. The nineteenth century saw an enormous increase in the size of Kensington's population. The nurseries and market gardens were replaced by countless city streets, as

the village was engulfed by a new suburbia. Spearheaded once again by the inexhaustible Norman Shaw, the late 1880s saw the open spaces of Earl's Court transformed into squares of red-brick mansion blocks, the nurseries and market produce soon to be available from quite another venue, the establishment of Harrods shopping emporium.

Addison Road, running along the western boundary of the Holland Estate, was the first to be developed; building began in 1824 and continued on and off for over thirty years, resulting in a mix of modest terraces of late Georgian houses and grander Victorian mansions. The northern boundary was also targeted and architects William and Francis Radford were commissioned by the fourth Lord Holland to build eighty large detached houses in a horseshoe shape, with a central mews and stables. The tree-lined streets of Holland Park, together with the stucco villas of Campden Hill Square, remain some of the grandest in London.

Today the designation "Kensington" is used to describe an area which loosely encompasses streets as far west as the exhibition centre at Olympia, the squares of red-brick mansion blocks in Earl's Court and much of the property towards South Kensington. With Holland Park, Hyde Park and Kensington Gardens all close at hand, Kensington is still considered to be one of the most desirable areas of London in which to live, and is commensurately one of the villages with the grandest, most imposing and expensive residences. Less Bohemian than Notting Hill, the antique shops of Kensington Church Street represent Kensington's more traditional

This stately series of columned entrances (right) graces a Victorian mansion block in Cadogan Square in Chelsea. Appearances can be misleading however, for other residential façades disguise more commercial enterprises—a restaurant and bistro in Queen's Gate in South Kensington (far left) and a local pub in Chelsea, decked out with window boxes and hanging baskets (above).

A skate-boarder strikes a pose on the steps leading up to the Royal Albert Hall (above) flanked by cherry trees whose blossoms carpet the steps in the springtime.

atmosphere, while the shops, boutiques and pubs around the High Street, together with some of its fashionable restaurants, attract younger generations from all over town.

South Kensington developed in the 1850s following Prince Albert's wish that there should be an area set aside for culture and education. Thus, the next fifty years gave rise to a number of museums, including the Natural History Museum, the Victoria & Albert Museum and the Royal Albert Hall.

Located within the Borough of Kensington & Chelsea, today there is little to distinguish South Kensington from these two main villages in either its style of architecture or the lifestyle of its residents. Yet, it is probably the one area of London where conversations in French will be heard more frequently than in English. The site of the French Lycée, several food shops and patisseries, along with a bookshop and

A pleasing symmetry is achieved (left) by the mirror image of the double bay windows in this mansion block in Herbert Crescent, Knightsbridge.

newsagent selling French publications, lend neighbouring Bute Street and Harrington Road a Parisian flavour.

CHELSEA

If Kensington was known as "the old court suburb", Chelsea was "the village of palaces". Its original focus was the Old Church (rebuilt in 1956), in the early 1500s a place of worship for Sir Thomas More, whose statue graces the Embankment. The Duke of Norfolk, the Earl of Shrewsbury and even Henry VIII himself had beautiful residences built in the village.

Arguably Chelsea's most famous monument, the Royal Hospital was begun in 1682 by Sir Christopher Wren as a home for old soldiers. To this day it is still associated with those who served their country and the distinctive red uniforms of the Chelsea Pensioners colour the village's contemporary tapestry. Royal Avenue, a wide tree-lined boulevard also laid out in the 1680s, was designed to connect the Royal Hospital with Kensington Palace. It never got further than the King's Road and, until 1830, the King's Road was actually just that—a private road for the King to take him from Kensington Palace and the Royal Hospital to Hampton Court or Kew. In 1913 the grounds of the hospital held the first Chelsea Flower Show, and continue to be the site of the spectacle each May.

Cheyne Walk, named after the family who were lords of the manor from 1660 to 1712 is probably the most beautiful street in Chelsea. Set back from the Thames, this

Topiary box in ornate stone urns flank the steps to the grand front door of this Georgian house on Cheyne Walk. A blue plaque, the accolade awarded by English Heritage to properties in which famous people have resided, announces that this was once the home of the celebrated author, George Eliot.

street of Queen Anne houses, still miraculously preserved, has silently witnessed some of the eccentric lives of Chelsea's more decadent inhabitants.

Chelsea's appeal as a fashionable resort began in the mid-seventeenth century with the introduction of coffee houses. That of Cheyne Walk was established by James Salter, barber and former servant of Sir Hans Sloane. Known as Don Saltero's, the coffee house was also a curious museum full of bizarre objects, many of them given to Salter by Sloane himself.

Chelsea's artistic reputation began in the eighteenth century with the Chelsea Porcelain Works, and its fame as a home for artists was sealed in the nineteenth century with the arrival of J. M. W. Turner and John Martin.

In 1834, writer Thomas Carlyle moved into Cheyne Row, a narrow street of charming Queen Anne houses just behind Cheyne Walk, where he was visited by nearly every literary celebrity of the day. In 1862, the status of the neighbourhood was changed overnight by the arrival of Dante Gabriel Rossetti, an original member of the Pre-Raphaelite Brotherhood, who moved into 16 Cheyne Walk and set up house with George Meredith and Algernon Swinburne. For the next decade, the house was a meeting place for poets and artists, their discussions punctuated by the sharp calls of the peacocks Rossetti kept in his garden.

The construction of Chelsea Embankment in 1870 destroyed the last vestige of the old riverside village, its wharves and taverns cleaned up and gentrified, providing

When spring arrives in London, riotous, thick ropes of wisteria wrap themselves around the iron railings and balustrades of houses, carpeting façades with a needlepoint of white, mauve and darker purple, whether in one of the tiny streets of colourful cottages which lead into the King's Road (left) or the grander façade of a house on Cheyne Walk in Chelsea (right).

Victorian architects with an opportunity to experiment. Norman Shaw and Philip Webb were at the forefront of Chelsea's red-brick revolution, which saw mansion blocks go up behind Cheyne Walk from Cheyne Gardens and Flood Street to Tite Street and part of Royal Hospital Road.

Artists and writers flocked to Chelsea, but soon its Bohemian flavour attracted more affluent residents, pushing out those that had given the village its character. Artists decamped, concentrating their attention on the studios built in the late nineteenth century in Tite Street, between the Royal Hospital and the Physic Garden. It was here that Oscar Wilde is reputed to have written his best work. Others moved to Glebe Place or into garrets and rooms dotted around the village.

The popular image of Chelsea today is still of a pretty village of brightly painted

$\mathbb{A}$n unexpected flash of bright colour catches the eye at the end of a cul-de-sac off the King's Road (right) where many of the small cottages which line Bywater Street have been painted in blues and mauves.

Blue abounds in Chelsea, especially on these cottages in Godfrey Street (above). Others make do with a bright front door or a nearby red letterbox for a burst of colour.

artisans' cottages, studios and houseboats, where residents have the freedom of self-expression. Yet there is a smarter side to Chelsea, reflected in the gracious squares and tree-lined streets of semi-detached houses and the grandiose white stucco villas of The Boltons. Built in the 1850s around an oval garden and the church of St Mary's, these freehold properties were designed to attract wealthy Victorians. The square, together with its surrounding streets of imposing residences, continues to

appeal to the affluent and puts this part of Chelsea on a par with Kensington.

There is also a more street-wise side, controlled by its central artery, the King's Road, into which all roads, squares, terraces and mews eventually run. London's first trendy boutique was opened here, establishing the King's Road as a centre of alternative culture. By the mid-1950s, bars, shops and jazz clubs were sprouting up all over Chelsea and the "Chelsea Set" were a force to be reckoned with. As the trend-setters began to settle down, new demands were generated. The most enduring proved to be an interest in home design—Terence Conran opened the first Habitat store on the King's Road in the mid-1960s and has never looked back.

<A> lone oarsman prepares his scull for a practice session. The upper reaches of the Thames, particularly around the bridges of Hammersmith and Putney, are home to several rowing clubs and inter-club rivalry is intense. The sculls are stored like sardines in special boathouses near the banks of the river.

RICHMOND

Away from the cut and thrust of modern London, one or two villages are far enough removed to be considered towns in their own right.

Richmond, to the south-west, is the only borough to span both banks of the Thames. Originally a fishing hamlet with a simple manor house, the area caught the eye of several early monarchs and in the time of Henry VII, when the manor house was transformed into a palace, the fate of Richmond became inextricably linked with that of the royal household.

Pomp and circumstance encouraged people to move out of London and join the court circle, creating a heritage of manor houses and wonderful gardens *en route*. Gracious estates once stretched the length of the river between London and Hampton Court. Those that remain catalogue an extraordinary architectural diversity: Syon House, seat of the Dukes of Northumberland since 1594 and improved by successive generations; Ham House, built on a Jacobean H-Plan in 1610; Osterley Park, an eighteenth-century reconstruction of a

Tudor building; Marble Hill House, an eighteenth-century Palladian villa and Chiswick House, modelled on Palladio's Villa Rotunda by the third Earl of Burlington in 1725.

In Richmond itself, the finest examples of this royal legacy are the Queen Anne terraces and early eighteenth-century houses which can be found elegantly adorning the village green—Maids of Honour Row, Old Palace Terrace and Old Palace Place— tucked discreetly back from the main high street of contemporary shops and offices. Richmond Palace, the birthplace of Henry VIII, has long since gone, but the gateway to the Green, beside Maids of Honour Row, remains, together with the restored buildings of the Wardrobe behind it.

Contemporary residents, as the wealthy merchants before them, prefer the view from Richmond Hill, while the legacy of late Georgian and Victorian houses provide ample opportunity for those seeking a certain anonymity not far from the hurly-burly of town.

<L>ondon is awash with cherry blossoms in the early spring, the pink and white petals bringing a welcome touch of colour to the strictness of the clipped green hedges and black iron railings which enclose many small front gardens.

The picturesque, clapboard exterior and small garden encircled by a wooden picket fence encapsulate the rural idyll, yet this house in Dulwich is less than half an hour from central London (on a good day!).

DULWICH

As far removed from Richmond as is geographically possible and yet still within London, Dulwich on the south-east edge of the city has been compared to a Hampshire village in its style and atmosphere. It would probably have remained a quiet, insular village cut off from the main stream if it were not for Dulwich College. Endowed by the actor Edward Alleyn, and completed in 1618, Dulwich College was constantly short of funds and its buildings in need of restoration throughout the eighteenth century. Nineteenth-century England saw a renewed interest in education, and the College received a bequest of paintings which put it on the road to financial recovery. Architect Sir John Soane, designed a gallery in the village to house the collection. Built in 1811, it is one of the first purpose-built picture galleries in England and includes a mausoleum for its benefactors. The present Dulwich College, which bears no resemblance to its ancestor, was designed by Charles Barry and built in rich red brick. It was reopened in 1870.

Dulwich Village has lost none of its early charm. The visitor's imagination is captivated by the white-painted picket fences of a bygone era. Neat lawns are punctuated by white bollards linked with smart chain, while large eighteenth-century houses stand in substantial gardens screened by tall trees from the prying eyes of passers-by. Meadows, parks and vast expanses of green stretch away on all sides. The sudden formality of a set of tennis courts and the Victorian roof of a wooden cricket pavilion temper this extraordinary feeling of having momentarily wandered into a village in the middle of the country.

PARKS AND GARDEN

The surface of the Long Water in Kensington Gardens (preceding page) glistens in the sunshine, while water pours from the upturned vessel held by a beautiful stone maiden in the Italian Gardens.

Few of the world's major cities can claim as many central parks as London. There is hardly a street which is not lined with trees or a residential square which does not serve as a communal garden at its centre. Roof terraces, balconies, window boxes, plants in pots and hanging baskets: the English love of gardens and of green spaces is manifested through every conceivable alternative. London, despite its overcrowded streets and the inevitable pollution associated with a metropolis of its size, is certainly greener than most cities.

Walking is, without doubt, one of the best ways to discover a city and, to know London well, a stroll through its parks is essential. The gardens are freely accessible to the public for all sorts of activities: roller-blading, horse-riding, swimming, jogging or simply enjoying a family picnic.

These parks and gardens fall into three main categories. The Royal Parks, of which there are ten, are the oldest; they have evolved from the hunting grounds of generations of royal families and the private lands attached to many of their residences, such as Kensington Palace or Hampton Court.

Next are the gardens of historic houses, which would once have been country estates outside London, now swallowed up in the metropolis. These include Osterley Park, Ham House, Syon Park and Chiswick House to the west and Kenwood to the north.

Finally, there are the specialist working gardens such as the Royal Botanic Gardens at Kew, the Chelsea Physic Garden and the Tradescant Garden (or Museum of Garden History) for which public access is restricted to certain times of the year.

Add to this the plethora of common land, heath, open grassland and garden squares, which are dotted all over central London, together with the fantastic variety of private gardens, from the size of a pocket handkerchief to areas as vast as an acre or more, and the secret of London's greenness is largely revealed. The rest is down to the English weather.

Summer has arrived in London and a local cricket team disports itself on the club's grounds at Kew Green, south of the Thames, (top left) while further on in the botanical gardens, a family takes a detour from the path that winds through the wildflowers and enjoys a rest on a bench in the shade (right).

On the opposite bank of the river a little further downstream, the gardens surrounding Chiswick House are in full bloom and the wonderful conservatory is curtained in wisteria (bottom left).

PARKS

The Royal Parks are "gardens for the gardenless", as different in size, structure and location as in the diverse attractions they each have to offer. Walled or surrounded by ornamented iron fencing, with imposing gateways, all Royal Parks are closed during the hours of darkness.

Greenwich is the oldest of the Royal Parks, its palace the birthplace of Mary I and Elizabeth I, and was frequently used for

jousting and banquets in Tudor times. Queen's House was completed in 1635 and the foundation stone for the Royal Observatory laid in 1675. The celebrated Royal Naval College, originally planned by Charles II as a palace, but with only one wing constructed, was completed by Wren and Hawksmoor toward the end of the seventeenth century. The park has been open to the public since the eighteenth century and is as famous for its rare trees as it is for its beautiful buildings. Today it is celebrated for one of the best views over London.

St James's Park (left and right) lies in the heart of London. Its ornamental lake designed by John Nash is home to numerous birds, including a group of resident pelicans. With Buckingham Palace at the western end of the lake, this view east from the pedestrian bridge, which spans the middle of the water, shows Duck Island and beyond to Horse Guards. The blossom from the many cherry trees which surround the lake litters the grass like confetti after a wedding.

St James's Park is London's most central green space and occupies ninety-three acres stretching away from Buckingham Palace. Distinguished today by its lake and statuesque pelicans, it has been the backdrop to four centuries of pomp and circumstance.

The Mall runs the length of its northern boundary and for 150 years was a fashionable promenade, originally used as the alley for a game of Pell Mell (or *paille mall*) a favourite pastime of seventeenth-century noblemen. Its tree-lined distinctive red Tarmac road is still decked out with flags for State visits and is used by the Queen and the royal family on State occasions. The park's location makes it a natural honey pot for tourists wanting a glimpse of the royal family, but during the heady days of summer, lunch time also brings out office workers, stealing a swift half an hour of sunshine away from their desks.

Green Park, on the north-west side of the palace is surprisingly urban by contrast, with few organised flower beds and a noticeable lack of colour. Only disorderly banks of daffodils create an unexpected splash of yellow amidst the tall plane trees in early spring. The park is said to have once been the burial ground for lepers from a hospital which was rebuilt in the seventeenth century as St James's Palace— a possible, though fanciful, explanation for the absence of floral colour. Sheep are reported to have grazed here as late as 1948, in the lee of such grand properties as The Ritz and Spencer House, but today the wildlife is limited to the occasional squirrel and strutting pigeon.

Winter's end is heralded by sunshine and trees in blossom at St James's Park. Tourists and Londoners alike will soon be out to take advantage of this brief spell of good weather (left).

Even this romantically inspired face on an urn in Kensington's Italian Gardens seems to bask happily in the sun (left).

Hyde Park now covers a mere 360 acres but as the hunting grounds for Henry VIII, it would have extended as far as Hampstead Heath. When William III came to live at Kensington Palace at the end of the seventeenth century, he hung three hundred lamps from the branches of the trees which lined the *route du roi* (hence Rotten Row) from the palace to St James's. It was thus the first road in England to be lit at night.

In 1730 William Kent created the Serpentine by damming six connecting pools, fed by the Westbourne River. The mood of the lake changes with the seasons. At summer's close, when the boats are moored in groups beneath the bridge and then finally removed for repair and storage, a hardy group of swimmers, reputed to be the oldest bathing club in England, get together and break the early morning ice of the Serpentine.

A long-standing club tradition requires a swim on Christmas Day.

Flowers were not planted in Hyde Park until 1860. Today's design boasts the formality of pleached lime trees, rose arbours and well-stocked beds of flowers in the Rose Garden, near the Queen Elizabeth Gate. They attract as many visitors as the banks of impromptu spring crocuses, snowdrops, daffodils and bluebells which fill the park with colour, as the first tentative green

softens the gaunt shapes of the trees in spring.

The park is no longer grazed, sheep having been replaced some time ago by the mechanical mower. Yet, over the last few years the grass has been allowed to grow long during the summer, in a return to the husbandry of earlier times. Grass pathways are cut through the longer vegetation, reinstating the original walks, while broad swathes of lawn are mown on either side of the gravel walkways. A lush growth is left around the base of the trees and through the groves, encouraging the resurgence of

native wildflowers and the re-introduction of indigenous wildlife. A conducive spot to spend romantic summer evenings with a chilled bottle of champagne, a picnic basket and a rug to ward off the evening chill, it is easy to forget that one is in the heart of London. When August draws to a close the long grass is finally harvested and the meadows along Rotten Row are dotted with haystacks.

Two low-flying geese cruise past Watts' Statue of Physical Energy on their regular early morning patrol of **Kensington Gardens.** Adjoining Hyde Park—not to be confused as part of it—Kensington Gardens is a mere 275 acres. More formal and with a genteel charm, plans for its design were first drawn up in 1720 with extensive park land east of Kensington Palace devised while George I was still alive. In those days it would have been surrounded by market gardens. Today, some of London's most expensive properties overlook its beautiful avenues.

The lines of trees which form the avenues leading from the Round Pond in an easterly direction were planted in the early nineteenth century. Everywhere one looks there are vistas and avenues, statues and water.

The Round Pond is situated close to Kensington Palace. A daily source of inspiration to joggers and dog-walkers alike, it is home to the Gardens' resident swans, a skein circling noisily overhead, their wing beats slow and ponderous as they describe a perfect arc, landing with comic dignity on the surface of the pond. William and Mary are the most famous breeding pair, showing

Overlooking the Long Water, the Italian Gardens, with a series of exuberant fountains, is an unexpected delight to come across when strolling through the north-west corner of Kensington Gardens (left and below).

The surrounding ornate stone wall, embellished with garlanded urns and romantic statues lends a touch of formality to the lush setting of the Italian Gardens (right).

off a long line of cygnets every year. The family nestles in the long grass shaded by some convenient tree as summer progresses. Groups of green and white striped deck chairs come out as Easter approaches, the weekends busy with sun-seekers and Londoners in search of fresh air.

Formality reasserts itself in the shape of the Italian Water Gardens at the top of the Long Water. Inspired by the Petit Trianon at Versailles, it is a wonderfully excessive display of fountains, basins, canals, balustrades, vases and statues.

The Albert Memorial, at the southern edge of the Gardens, was designed by George Gilbert Scott and erected in 1872. The statue of Prince Albert by John Foley, has been shrouded in protective scaffolding during eight years of restoration. The memorial is slowly shedding its skin, like a butterfly emerging from a lengthy incarceration. Its gilded cross glitters brightly above the tree tops, a reminder of all that Prince Albert contributed to the arts and sciences during his lifetime. A long and popular flower walk, with a large assortment of trees and shrubs, extends for 700 yards behind the memorial.

By the Victorian era, Kensington Gardens was the natural place to which

The striped seats of abandoned deck chairs are teased by a passing breeze as a late-afternoon chill descends on the Round Pond in Kensington Gardens—a spot dear to Henry James's heroine Maisie.

nannies brought their charges and it still holds a magical quality for children to this day. The garden will be forever associated with J. M. Barrie's wonderful tale of *Peter Pan*. In 1912, a statue of the boy hero, by Sir George Frampton, was put up in the gardens at dead of night. In keeping with the character's mystery, it seemed to appear in the morning as if by magic. In 1928, the Elfin Oak, a tree stump carved with small animals by Ivor Innes, was set up together with the playground at the northwest corner of the park. The original swings in the playground were a gift from J. M. Barrie.

Regent's Park started life at the beginning of the nineteenth century when the whole area north of Marylebone Road was laid out by the architect John Nash as an exclusive residential area with elegant buildings arranged in a park.

It is a complex creation, arranged in two concentric circles: an inner one with gardens and an outer one with terraces, stucco crescents and handsome buildings. The inner ring, once occupied by the Garden of the Royal Botanical Society has now been replaced by Queen Mary's Rose Garden.

The strange, barren rocks of the Mappin Terraces and the sculptural shape of the aviary, designed by Lord Snowdon, at London Zoo are clearly visible from many points in the park. A favourite of adults and children alike, the Zoological Society was founded in 1826 and its collection of animals opened to the public two years later, on a site designed by architect Decimus Burton.

For the really young members of the public, for whom the zoo is a little daunting, Regent's Park has a series of man-made

One of many broad, tree-lined avenues in Kensington Gardens, this majestic path leads up to the gates of Kensington Palace.

lakes, home to a great variety of birds. Here prams and pushchairs crowd the water's edge as little children throw fistfuls of bread crumbs to the overweight residents.

A sweep of the Regent's Canal passes along the park's northern boundary where more birds and other wildlife compete with the occasional barge and houseboat. The tow paths and bridges along its length, also designed by Nash, are a riot of cow parsley and wildflowers in the summer.

Behind the zoo rises Primrose Hill; its summit 206 feet above sea level gives breathtaking views over St Paul's Cathedral and Westminster Abbey. The primroses have long since gone, although efforts have been made to recreate an environment conducive to their growth, and in the mean time, the hill has become popular with keen kite flyers.

Richmond Park is by far the largest of the Royal Parks at a mighty 2,400 acres, with thousands of indigenous trees and a spread of unbroken country. The coppices and stretches of ground covered in bracken, where herds of red and fallow deer roam freely, are virtually the same as in the seventeenth century. The oaks are particularly old and, with those of Epping Forest, represent the survivors of the medieval forests which once surrounded London. The trunks of fallen giants litter the woods, the lightning-blasted stumps of others, reminiscent of drawings by Arthur Rackham, add character and mystery to a park of surprising wildness.

There are no fountains or statues here, for Richmond has escaped the civilisation of the other London parks. It was created

by Charles I, who forced landowners to sell up so that he would have a place to escape to. Today a brick wall still exists, with access gained through six carriage and five pedestrian gates.

Sidmouth Wood, the largest of many, was planted in 1823 with oaks, beeches and sweet chestnuts. It is a bird sanctuary, essentially closed to walkers, with one path permitted through its centre. The Pen Ponds, former gravel pits full of pink roach, carp and gudgeon, were formed in the eighteenth century and reserved for anglers. Today they are home to ducks, swans, moorhens and numerous other birds.

The list of activities is endless. Richmond Park has something for everyone: golf, mountain bikes, stables, exclusive plantations of flora and fauna, short walks for wobbly toddlers and long walks for tireless hounds. A short car journey from the centre of London, it is the extraordinary juxtaposition of high-rise flats on the park's perimeter with herds of grazing deer and children at play, which makes the rural atmosphere of Richmond Park so enjoyable.

Large enough to get lost in and with areas of dense wood and open grassland, Richmond Park allows Londoners the opportunity to pursue their various sports, even the most unusual of city hobbies, falconry (above).

In direct contrast to this apparent wilderness is the immaculate design of Regent's Park (below, Sussex Terrace), inspired by John Nash, who designed the park, encircling it with gracious terraces and lawns.

Further up river, **Hampton Court** has magnificent and gracious gardens which have been recently redesigned to echo the original plans of the grand formal avenues and ornamental water fountains laid out by John Rose in the seventeenth century.

avenue of horse chestnut trees sixty feet wide and one mile long. Under William III, who had been so innovative in Hyde Park, the gardens at Hampton Court became the Great Fountain Garden, famous for its huge yew trees.

Deer graze peacefully in the vastness of Richmond Park, while a game of football is played on the meadow immediately behind the herd (right) .

A detail of wisteria against the wall of the Orangery in the grounds of Ham House, situated west of London, just outside Richmond (following page). Also at Ham House a view through the yew hedge into the Cherry Garden (page 59). A statue of Bacchus stands at the centre of the garden, which has been created using dwarf box and clipped box cones, with alternating santolina and lavender in the centre of each bed.

Gardener to Charles II, Rose's design was another English attempt to emulate Versailles. Hampton Court Palace was significantly extended by Sir Christopher Wren and neighbouring Bushey Park was incorporated into his grand scheme, with a design for a processional route to the north façade of the palace, down a magnificent

Hampton Court was first opened to the public by Queen Victoria in 1837, the year of her coronation. Visitors can admire the Black Hamburg vine, known as the Great Vine, which was planted in 1768, and yields about seven hundred pounds of grapes a year. The grapes are sold to the public in August, while in early July Hampton Court

holds its own flower show to rival that of Chelsea.

While the English monarchs were installed at Hampton Court, many aristocratic families constructed residences nearby. Some of these, built along the banks of the Thames, are still standing and open to the public today. One of the most interesting is **Ham House,** a mansion built in 1610 to the west of Richmond, just beyond the boundary of the Royal Park. Its rooms still filled with original furniture and textiles, the property has recently undergone a complete restoration under the direction of the National Trust. The gardens and grounds have also been restored in part to their original seventeenth-century layout and incorporate the formality of the Cherry Garden within areas of orchard and wilderness.

Holland Park near the heart of Kensington was originally part of the estate belonging to Holland House, a Jacobean mansion built in 1606. The property enjoyed a chequered history and with the Victorian building boom in 1866, lands to the north and west were sold off. The house, severely damaged during World War II, was taken over by the London City Council in 1952. The ground floor and arcades were restored, along with the east wing, where open-air concerts and plays are performed in what has become known as the Court Theatre. The grounds surrounding the house are made up of three formal gardens: the Rose Garden, Iris Garden and Dutch Garden, where the first dahlias ever to have grown in England are reputed to have been planted by Lady Holland. The

Garden Ballroom has been converted into a restaurant, while art exhibitions are held in the former Orangery and the restored ice house.

Battersea Park, south of the Thames, enjoys no royal nor aristocratic status. Its two hundred acres fronting the river were once the preferred location for illegal shooting contests. In 1851 the swampy land

Holland Park, in the centre of Kensington, is blessed with majestically mature trees (top right) and several formal gardens which bloom with vibrant colour during the summer months (bottom right). Surrounded on all sides by houses, Holland Park is popular with families and is always full of life. The Orangery can be glimpsed through the lush shrubbery (left).

was purchased by the government and filled in with earth taken from the docks. To enliven an otherwise flat park, mounds and hillocks were constructed, a lake was excavated and a sub-tropical garden laid out.

A royal coat of arms, picked out in gilt, adorns the black iron gates at one of the entrances to Kew Gardens (above).

BOTANICAL GARDENS

While the Royal Parks were planted with species that would make for a lovely landscape, the botanical gardens served as outdoor laboratories, emphasising variety and rarity. Often associated with medical schools, their main purpose was for botanical studies. Today, many of these exotic gardens are open to the general public.

The Royal Botanic Gardens at Kew are shrouded in a certain mystery, secluded and private behind their high brick wall. A place of beauty and wonderful variety, this is a setting where people can roam at will from organised, formal gardens to near wilderness. Developed from an extraordinary collection of exotic plants owned by Augusta, widow of Frederick Prince of Wales (the son of George II), Kew Gardens has come to be regarded as the botanical centre of the world.

Running alongside the upper reaches of the Thames, with man-made lakes frequented by ducks, black swans and other wildfowl, Kew is popular with picnickers, avid walkers, families out to explore, and botanical *aficionados* alike. A native woodland, awash with bluebells in early May, an azalea garden and magnolia walk, gardens and herbaceous borders for every season,

bizarre follies and immense greenhouses, are sufficient to keep the most demanding gardener interested.

Alongside the experts and those passionate about rhododendrons, cacti or palm trees are others who come to Kew Gardens to enjoy a certain outdoor solitude. The water-colourist sits on an isolated bench in a sea of long grass, her fair skin protected by a large-brimmed straw hat, intent on her work in the shade of a Weeping Hornbeam. Students with heavy piles of books quietly revise for the summer exams, enjoying a stolen afternoon of unexpected warmth and sunshine in a glade of beech trees where the last of the bluebells catches a shaft of sunlight. A group of young children surreptitiously

The houses along Swan Walk tower over the high brick wall which encircles the Chelsea Physic Garden and its burgeoning beds of plants, flowers and trees (below).

In the Kew Gardens nursery, young plants and seedlings are nurtured in greenhouses until they come of age (above).

feed the geese and ducks with the remains of their lunch in an atmosphere of relaxation and calm.

Another source of fascinating and unusual plants, is the **Tradescant Garden,** named after two seventeenth-century royal gardeners. Near Lambeth Palace on the south bank of the Thames, it occupies the site of the former churchyard of St Mary's, a disused church which was rescued in 1976. Now known as the Museum of Garden History, the churchyard has been transformed into a knot garden with low hedges of thyme, rosemary and dwarf box set in formal squares.

More surprising still is the **Chelsea Physic Garden,** founded in 1673 by the Worshipful Society of Apothecaries of London and designed for botanical instruction, it is nearly one hundred years older than Kew. Situated close to the Thames, so that river barges could bring students to rural Chelsea from the City of London, the Physic Garden is still involved with the research of medicinal plants. Bought in 1712 by Sir Hans Sloane at the same time as the Manor of Chelsea, the four-acre site was leased in perpetuity to the Apothecaries for the princely sum of five pounds per annum. It is the one of the oldest botanical gardens in England, and enclosed by its seventeenth-century brick walls, seems little changed by the centuries.

Specialists and amateurs, their curiosity excited by the secret garden, tour the orderly beds of plants and flowers, which are painstakingly annotated and meticulously groomed. While some visitors are immersed in animated discussion over a bed

As a gentle breeze blows in off the Thames, it is time to take a break in a withdrawn corner of wilderness in Kew Gardens (above).

of multi-coloured irises, others make for the open lawn, where they spread rugs and open the Sunday newspapers.

OUTDOOR DIVERSIONS

Alternatives to gardens, where Londoners can stroll and take the air, can be found in the variety of Hampstead Heath, its hilly terrain encouraging hardy walkers as well as those ambling between Jack Straw's Castle and The Spaniard, two pubs neatly positioned for the lazier fraternity. Nearby Kenwood House, situated in its own grounds, offers the additional pleasure of outdoor concerts in the summer.

The city's cemeteries have also long been popular for quiet walks, many of them informal with stylised arrangements of tombs, mausoleums and terraced catacombs, where the grass in summer grows long and free, cats sunbathe on the warm gravestones and, in Highgate Cemetery, the occasional tourist can be found crouched in admiration before the final resting place of Christina Rossetti or George Eliot.

It is an inherent talent for gardening and growing things which the English have

Enclosed by the assorted buildings which make up this unusual property in south-east London, sculptor and designer, Oriel Harwood (right), currently fills the courtyard which separates home from workshop with work in progress. One day a vast wooden elephant will replace the table and chairs in the centre and her simple workshop will be given a classical façade.

For city-dwellers without a private garden, London's Victorian cemeteries (right) offer a peaceful alternative. The gravestones and monuments are often overgrown with ivy, and the grass is allowed to grow long in the summer.

So many of London's gardens are havens of peace, hidden from the public gaze. A few have views over Regent's Canal in Islington (below).

fallen back on in times of trouble and hardship. During the Second World War, when there was a paucity of all things edible, Londoners and other city-dwellers were encouraged to grow vegetables on patches of common land, wherever anything could be persuaded to take root. Known as allotments, these tiny portions of land, often handed down through the family, are still very much in demand today, the assorted patchwork of vegetable and flower gardens a part of the suburban countryside. Garden sheds, bamboo canes supporting runner beans and sweet peas, rows of tomatoes, dahlias and chrysanthemums—the allotments offer the first hint of the country to the exhausted commuter gazing out of the train window on his way out of London. At weekends, entire families, or fathers intent on an afternoon's peace and quiet, while away the time, either working on the plot or snoozing in a deck chair.

It is probably many of these same people who swell the queues thronging into the grounds of the Royal Hospital every May for the last days of the Chelsea Flower Show, when it is open to the general public. Considered to be the world's most prestigious flower show, it has a marquee which covers three and a half acres. Filled to capacity every year with exhibits ranging from examples of the most beautiful cut flowers, to herbs, Bonsai trees and stands offering advice on dealing with garden pests, late afternoon on the last day throws up endless bargains for those prepared to battle for them. As the show draws to a close the contents of the stands and the numerous complete gardens, which have been temporarily

Cadogan Gardens (top) is shared by local residents. The tempting garden is overlooked by three of Chelsea's most charming small hotels.

Those with less space are content to festoon the façades of their houses with wisteria and creeper and to grow shrubs in terracotta pots (bottom).

installed on the lawns surrounding the Royal Hospital, are put up for sale. The spoils could end up anywhere—from a suburban allotment to a city window box.

PRIVATE GARDENS

The secrecy surrounding many of London's residential properties is exaggerated by the number of protective gardens, thick hedges and tall fences. Many houses have courtyard gardens or expanses of lawn at the rear of the property, completely hidden from view and all the more unexpected. Apartment blocks may also share a communal garden, tended by a resident gardener. In addition, the majority of mansion blocks and terraced squares of apartments have private lawns and flower borders, their boundary fences lined with sweet-smelling lilac trees, magnolia and other delights, creating unexpected glimpses of colour between the red-brick buildings. While some will argue against this elitist privilege of a private communal garden, its luxury inevitably reflected in the purchase price of the property, the fact that there are so many garden squares and green spaces in London, not only ensures a greater privacy for flat-dwellers but also affords them access to the outdoors without the work involved in a garden's maintenance.

The voices of garden experts, however, have recently been joined by those of Lord Snowdon and Members of Parliament, in a general criticism of the way London's squares are maintained. Unlike the French, the English have a reserved attitude to pruning and many plants have been allowed to grow out of hand. The majority of trees in London's squares have become too large for the surrounding architecture, resulting in a loss of proportion and respect for the buildings. There are too many evergreens and gloomy laurels and a conscious lobby is now underway to reintroduce more indigenous plants and trees to the city.

General public awareness is also being increased by the work of a new charity called Flora and Fauna which is trying to encourage Londoners to grow native plants and flowers and to abandon the hybrids, in an attempt to bring back a balanced mix to the capital. A database is now available, advising which trees and plants are local to a particular district of London.

For the many London residents who are fortunate enough to have their own gardens, there is not only the problem of general maintenance but, initially, the creation of that perfect environment. Those who decide to tackle the challenge themselves find they have time for little else. Others opt for the gurus of outdoor style and take on a landscape gardener.

Londoners use their gardens for different purposes. They often need the extra space for entertaining, which encourages a more theatrical approach to garden design. Normally seen from a fixed viewpoint, looking out from the house, London gardens are essentially an outdoor room where walls and vertical surfaces have to be created to conceal their immediate surroundings: ugly buildings, rows of neighbours' windows, or a nearby main road.

Olga Polizzi's Italianate courtyard garden, designed by George Carter, is shielded on all sides by tall trees. The baroque folly at the rear adds to the charm of the space, which is ideal for entertaining, and a quiet retreat away from the bustle of London life.

George Carter, who believes that a garden needs lines that will give it structure, draws the eye to the back wall of Olga Polizzi's garden by placing an ornate trellis within a folly.

George Carter, one of the current favourites in gardening circles, finds the art of creating a London garden a unique discipline with challenges that he does not encounter in the countryside.

For George, scale is one of the most interesting factors when designing an urban garden. Emphasising the dramatic side of garden design, he has discovered that large objects can feature strongly without appearing ludicrously out of scale. The perspective of a garden can be intensified by the size of the objects within it.

One of George's favourite London gardens, in which he has successfully played with perspective, is situated in a secret courtyard behind the mews house of hotelier and interior designer Olga Polizzi. Olga enjoys entertaining and her garden is designed on a series of planes, like the wings of a stage set, which enhance the feeling of spaciousness. It divides into smaller rooms, in fact four dining rooms, which she has furnished with a variety of tables and chairs, creating separate, intimate areas.

For George Carter, it is important that an urban garden has a striking effect at night, thus in addition to candles in the dining area, Olga's garden is spotlit and backlit with great subtlety. Such clever use of light can transform a garden into an unreal world, flattening out the three dimensional and creating amazing shadows. George has problems with the classic free-form English garden which lacks framework. He believes that some controlling lines are necessary and that the best results are achieved when free planting takes place within a rigid design—a juxtaposition of

two very different disciplines. He draws inspiration from the great gardens of the seventeenth century, which were designed as stages for theatrical spectacles.

Used as a blank canvas, Londoners like to be able to change their gardens at will, whether for a particular party or to introduce a colour or theme. George Carter did just that in Olga Polizzi's garden. He introduced a new framework with topiary and abundant planting in the foreground, and designed the baroque folly against the back wall to hide the rows of blank windows

The double doors of Olga's dining room conservatory open on to the peaceful courtyard and the heady scent of lilies and Nicotiana.

which look down from the neighbouring apartment block. Looking out from the conservatory dining room, this small garden burgeons with plants and bold patches of green. The beds on either side spill over with luxuriant growth, terracotta pots of lilies, lavender and white Nicotiana fight for ground space with statues, marble body

parts and garden candles. The cypress trees are not only a reference to Olga's Italian origins, but also an indication of the surprising plants that will adapt to London's climate. Sheltered and several degrees warmer than the rest of the country, one can grow plants in London that would not survive anywhere else in England. Jasmine, palm trees, even banana palms have been known to enjoy the benefits of London air.

Lord Snowdon comes from a gardening family but disarmingly admits to knowing little if anything about plants. His London garden is an interesting mixture of formal planting and architectural design. An unwitting follower of George Carter's rule of thumb for formality, and allergic to any colours which stray from the tones of green and white, Snowdon has created a courtyard garden in which he likes to try out his latest designs.

Water plays an important part in his garden's layout, which revolves around a central fountain and circular pond upon which a group of faded French decoy ducks solemnly float. At the flick of a switch, water starts to spout from several orifices, including the eye sockets of a mask built into a garden wall, although Snowdon points out, there is a flaw in the simple design. Located under a deciduous tree, the shedding leaves fall into the mask, blocking the eyes and ruining the weeping effect. A plastic owl, concealed in the foliage of a recalcitrant tree is placed there to keep the pigeons away, but its hiding place is so overgrown that the birds fail to notice him.

Influenced by the work of his uncle, Oliver Messel, architecture has always been a passion for Lord Snowdon and his garden is testimony to his eye for design. Enclosed on one side by an extremely high wall and overlooked from behind by his neighbours' properties, he has incorporated his own house into the garden layout. Railings acquired from Ascot racecourse, dating from 1840 have been used around the perimeter, and the double doors to his photographic studio, which he has designed to resemble

Lord Snowdon's marvellous garden is the stage for his original creations. Water gurgles from a central fountain and spurts from the mouths and eyes of gargoyles scattered along the walls (left). A tranquil oasis, it is a place of peace and inspiration for Lord Snowdon, seen here leaning on an antique railing from the Ascot racecourse (right).

a Tasmanian railway station, open on to the garden. There is always a theatrical or humorous side to Snowdon's ideas. His latest scheme is a shed made of balsa wood and constructed specifically to fit into the corner of a garden. The design has been undergoing tests in the workshops at Chatsworth, and Snowdon hopes one day to have his corner shed installed in London.

Gardening itself is not of interest to him, so the clipped box hedges and formal planting are designed with low maintenance in mind. Nor does the idea of using the garden for idle pleasure appeal to Lord Snowdon, although he does confess to enjoying the occasional lunch *al fresco* if the English weather proves conducive.

John and Deborah James's garden in west London is an oasis of rural calm, in spite of being directly under the main flight path into Heathrow Airport. The area was formerly the archery butts for Syon House, seat of the Dukes of Northumberland, where orchards and kitchen gardens supplied some of London's fruit and vegetable markets until just before the First World War. It is still bordered on two sides by the wall to the original kitchen garden, now more or less entirely rebuilt, and several old apple trees—one identified as King of the Pippins—stand proudly in the centre.

Deborah inherited this Edwardian fantasy when she and her husband, the painter John James, bought the house some twelve years ago. Its maze of criss-crossing pathways, lawns and borders were totally overgrown and the terracing midway down the garden was hidden under bindweed,

bramble and ivy, its shape lost in an explosion of uncontrolled growth. Over the years, Deborah has worked to get back the original design; the result today is a country garden in the heart of an urban jungle. The veranda of the early nineteenth-century house is a mass of purple wisteria and climbing roses, with a pear tree and a white lilac gently scenting the terrace.

Deborah has tried to organise the garden in such a way that it has colour throughout the year. The tulips come first, followed by the roses and foxgloves and then nature simply takes over in an eruption of colour—bluebells, white tulips, forget-me-nots, a mass of pale blue and white. Deborah changes from pastel to gaudy on a whim. Centre stage is occupied by a winter flowering cherry tree, which spreads a wonderful pinkish-white blossom over the palette of colour on the ground. It starts flowering in November and gives a dappled shade throughout the summer. The terraces, constructed from old bricks and York stone, are planted with rosemary and

In the garden of John and Deborah James, a sunken path of red brick (left) winds its way through the border which overflows with Helebores, tulips, wallflowers and self-seeded foxgloves and bluebells (below). Almost engulfed in the foliage of a neighbouring tree is the potting shed (right), where the serious gardening is undertaken.

The reassuringly dark and cosy interior of a wagon (left) at the far end of the garden provides an unusual refuge from the elements and a momentary pause for Deborah in the daily battle with weeds and bramble which threaten to take over.

lavender. Further back into the garden is an area of unruly wilderness, separated from the borders by a sunken path of red brick. This section has changed dramatically since the demise of a huge Vibernum and, due to the terrible wet month of April, the Dog Violet, Wood Sorrel, Lords and Ladies, Primroses and Woody Nightshade have been engulfed by a mass of weeds.

The back of the garden is littered with a collection of strange objects. A narrow path beats a trail to a wagon parked under a protective awning; a short flight of wooden steps leads up to its front door. Painted a rich burgundy, the wagon has belonged to Deborah for more than twenty-five years. Here she comes to think and plan, write and drink tea. Nearby stands an old telephone box, at one time a feature in many of John James' paintings. The standard red stood out like a sore thumb at the end of the garden and, at Deborah's insistence, was finally painted a pale grey. The bus shelter is a new acquisition and forms a focal point at the end of the sunken path, providing a haven to sit and contemplate.

What might once have been a pastime for those fortunate enough to have a garden has blossomed into a national passion. Patios, terraces—wherever there is a bare patch of ground—are filled with terracotta pots of colour, while wisteria, jasmine and honeysuckle are trained to hide the unsightly exterior fixtures common to most British architecture. Sundays are spent in one of London's nurseries or garden centres, potting and experimenting, the results filling basement wells, narrow balconies and roof terraces with colour and perfume.

An eruption of colour and a garden heady with the scent of flowers and herbs (left and above) are the happy results of Deborah's hard work.

INTERIORS

A fire glows in the hearth, its reflected light enhancing the deep colour of the panelling in the drawing room (right) of this Georgian house in Spitalfields. The homeliness of the room is in marked contrast to the more traditional grandeur of the spacious Victorian drawing room (far right) which is dominated by a vast seventeenth-century Dutch painting of the Dutch and English fleet in a wooden frame which was originally created for Merton College, Oxford.

So much of what happens in London takes place behind closed doors, with windows swathed in lengths of fabric, shuttered, blinded, inaccessible. The English love their privacy. They protect their homes from prying eyes behind fences and hedges, screens of trees and beds of tall rose bushes. As the first of twilight's long shadows fall on London's streets and lamps are switched on in the gathering gloom of hitherto hidden interiors, an unknown world is temporarily opened up to the idle passer-by.

That short period when a room is illuminated, before curtains are drawn and blinds descend, the chance opening of a door for a small uniformed child returning home from school; these are the moments shared with strangers, offering a glimpse of an unknown lifestyle, that might reveal a certain sense of style, of the individuality of those living within.

The architectural variety in London fires the imagination with endless possibilities. Whether living in narrow Georgian splendour or in the vastness of a warehouse loft, a white stucco fronted villa or a small flat, one is spoilt for choice. London's streets are buzzing with ideas, specialists, opportunists and artists. Competition is intense and the variety limitless. The elements that give an interior its personal style can be bought, acquired or even copied from architectural salvage yards, junk shops, street markets, antique shops and designer boutiques.

The vivid blue walls of Diane Berger's former Chelsea dining room (preceding double page) set off a collection of George III mezzotints-on-glass and three decorated open armchairs of the same period.

THE GEORGIAN PERIOD (1714–1810)

Dennis Severs pushes the black front door which opens onto the dark narrow hallway of his home. The smell of oranges assails the senses. As your eyes become accustomed to the gloom, past and present seem unified under one roof. It is Christmas, and the hallway is decorated with branches of fir trees entwined with lengths of red satin ribbon. Candles give off a soft glow against

"Open the dining parlour door and look. The sitters have walked away, leaving behind only the material evidence of their presence," thus begins the tour of Dennis Severs's house in Spitalfields. The candle-lit kitchen table in the low-ceilinged basement (right), like the dining table in the room above it (left), is laden with Christmas fare.

the dark walls. The noise of a passing horse and carriage echo on the cobblestones outside. The house is very cold and you are drawn to the flickering flames of a welcoming fire in the front room, where a table groans under the weight of a Christmas repast, the chairs pushed back hastily,

Red satin ribbons and branches of fir festoon the black hallway and staircase and the smell of fresh fruit pervades the house.

the plates half-finished. Each of the rooms in this extraordinary house sets a similar scene: somebody has just left as you arrived. The sweet notes of a yellow canary in a gilded cage echo down from the master bedroom; a child cries noisily from the servants' quarters in the attic and a ticking clock serves as the heartbeat of the house.

Built in 1724, this house in Folgate Street, Spitalfields would have been lived in by a master silk weaver and his family. Salvaged from a near derelict state by Dennis Severs, Folgate Street has been his home for the last thirty years. The restoration was intuitive, each of the ten rooms in the house slept in and its soul listened to before Dennis made any structural or decorative decisions.

Dennis Severs moved to England from California in 1967. Having always been more impressed by the European world he knew from paintings than by his native

America, he immediately identified with London. Its history and intrigue drew him in, giving him a sense of belonging. When he bought the house, he moved in that same day. His few neighbours referred to the house on Folgate Street as "a restoration comedy" because he was totally possessed by his desire to restore its Georgian splendour.

A pile of clean socks waiting to be paired off occupies a large space on the divan in the parlour, testimony to a contemporary domesticity—this house is not just a stage for Dennis, he really lives here. Yet when he started opening it to the public, he decided to invent an authentic Georgian family to reside in it, taking care to move around unnoticed in his own home.

The house on Folgate Street is a refuge from the bustle of a twentieth-century capital. As you duck under the low doorway into the basement kitchen, Dennis's silhouette is outlined in a rustic chair against the fire, a steaming mug of tea in his hand—a sense of peace between house and man.

Back out on the cobbled street, darkness is falling at the end of a winter's afternoon. The atmosphere is vaguely sinister, the enveloping cold fog reminiscent of harder times. Nearly thirty years ago, this area surrounding a once flourishing fruit and vegetable market was due to be condemned. Many houses had stood empty for years, where once there would have been a family on each floor. Buildings in side streets were occupied by semi-derelict sweat-shops and a few elderly inhabitants

Upstairs on the landing a small circular table teeters under the weight of a tiered stand of sweets and delicacies, mirroring the candelabra that hangs above it.

The relative austerity of this writing corner by the window in a top-floor bedroom (above) contrasts sharply with the sumptuousness of the master bedroom (right). A collection of blue and white china vases dominates the wall above the fireplace. A small table is laid for breakfast.

hanging on to their tenancies, while others were used as brothels or shelters for alcoholics to spend the night.

The future of Spitalfields in the early 1970s lay in the balance; it took a certain courage to move to these cobbled streets of early Georgian houses. A few brave souls subscribed, however, attracted by the unique opportunity to restore a house which, due to the very poverty of the area over a period of two hundred years, had been left virtually untouched. At the time the inhabitants of Elder Street comprised a retired docker and his wife, a couple of elderly ladies, an informal brothel, a young solicitor, an Irish aristocrat and a renowned Marxist professor. The latter always attracted an interesting collection of people, the most memorable visit being one from the actress Vanessa Redgrave, who drew up outside his house one day in a white Rolls Royce.

Towards the end of the seventies, however, one side of the street ran into serious trouble. Having been acquired by property developers earlier in the decade, the row was threatened with demolition. Saved by the valiant efforts of the inhabitants of Elder Street, together with the support of various celebrities of the day, potential buyers had to be found quickly.

Angela Enthoven and her husband just happened to be in London at the time. A healer or medium by profession and with one foot, in a sense, permanently in the past, Angela has always been drawn to old houses. The couple had been concentrating their attention more on Wapping and the developing interest around the

Docklands, but were seduced by Elder Street and ended up buying two houses. The one they chose to live in is a splendid double-fronted, brick townhouse. A short flight of steps leads up to the front door, the house sectioned off from the narrow pavement by taut iron railings. This is a house of stature, a house of many parlours and "withdrawing rooms". The floorboards creak with age. There is a stillness, an air of expectancy, as if the house waits to assess its visitors. What human dramas could these walls relate? David Hockney is reputed to have said that he can never paint in London, for there are too many ghosts. Angela Enthoven does not seem to be happy unless there is at least one in her home. Everything here has a deeper, symbolic, almost ritual meaning. London has a long history and, Spitalfields, representative of old London, seems to attract outsiders seeking a new or different identity.

The restoration of Angela's house started from scratch and, since nothing had been removed and the fireplaces, staircase and wall panelling were all still original, it

In Spitalfields, the Enthoven's little house enchants all who enter. The original basement kitchen (above right) still retains its blackened range and granite flagged floor, although it is now used as the laundry room. Similarly simple in design is one of two small bathrooms in the attic (above).

Every room in the house has a soul. The drawing room (below) is sparsely furnished and almost monastic, while the cosy downstairs parlour (right) boasts the best fireplace in Spitalfields. The wall painting on the wooden panelling was adapted by Danny West from a French fabric. He was responsible for all the specialist paint work in the house.

An art historian specialising in interior decoration, Diane Berger chose the perfect Georgian house as a backdrop for her collection of period furniture. Soft red walls set off the decoration of this L-shaped drawing room: red silk curtains with crewel-work pelmets, a George III mahogany sofa covered in gros point floral needlework —all on bare polished floorboards (left).

was a relatively easy task. Like that of Dennis Severs, Angela's houses must have a soul and she now uses her healing skills on individual rooms, concentrating on removing any bad energy she finds there. So successful has she been that the atmosphere of Elder Street affects all who come to stay. Angela is encompassed by her house, cocooned and protected from the outside world, to which she returns each time with increasing reluctance. The house, in turn, needs to be loved and lived in, and now that

her family has grown up, she has finally decided to move on.

Other occupants of Elder Street see change as inevitable, although the Enthovens departure was marked by a deep sadness. The past will always be viewed with inevitable nostalgia, and yet the future, whatever it holds for this microcosm of historical London, is greeted with an air of excitement.

American **Diane Berger**, is also passionate about the Georgian period, and a near-derelict shell in a beautiful Chelsea square was to realise her dream and goal of re-creating and living in an authentic Georgian atmosphere.

Wellington Square is one of many residential squares, streets and mews which run into the King's Road, Chelsea's main artery. A colourful florist's barrow takes up daily residence at the entrance to the square, so banks of flowers regularly find their way to Diane's house. The square is narrow and intimate, the central garden adorned with a fountain amidst the lilac and tall plane trees ubiquitous to many London streets.

Diane is a perfectionist. When looking for a house, the period which interested her was narrow, from 1720 to 1790. She and her husband visited over two hundred period houses looking for one in which the architectural features were intact; Diane did not want a house which had been re-done. In order to recreate a complete Georgian atmosphere, they visited historic collections, stately homes and antique dealers, selecting furniture and architectural detail carefully. Those items that they were unable to find, Diane had recreated by English craftsmen. The decorative scheme for each room was either built around one object or dictated by the period colours of the furniture. Nothing was neglected, no detail considered too insignificant. They were to live in a Georgian museum.

The interior is unexpectedly colourful, the only panelling a creation of Diane's in the library, and this is a subdued soft grey. The hall is a yellow print room, the dining room a resonant blue.

Upstairs on the first floor, the L-shaped drawing room is red. Her bedroom and adjoining bathroom are rose, the hangings for the four-poster bed and free-standing bath, antique toile de Jouy. She has even painted the kitchen floor to resemble an Aubusson carpet.

The love affair would appear to be over, however. The couple have outgrown the house in Wellington Square, overcome by

a sense of claustrophobia and lack of individuality in the classic layout and design of these period London properties. The Georgian furniture acquired with such dedication, the paintings and fabrics, everything down to the cutlery has been sold under the hammer at a Christie's auction. London is never static. Properties come and go, its residents grow restless, become speculative or simply move on. The scene is constantly changing, with new opportunities in new areas.

An amusing touch (below) is the modern doll's house which is used as a drinks cabinet.

Another view of the L-shaped drawing room (above) in which a pair of Queen Anne walnut side chairs and a black and gilt chest decorated with Chinoiserie figures are key pieces.

Diane's bedroom is dominated by a mahogany four-poster bed with red toile de Jouy hangings and red and white silk damask curtains with toile de Jouy pelmets (right). The detail (above) shows the yellow-ribbed silk cover of one of the two side-tables which flank the sofa in the drawing room.

Diane and her husband moved to St Katherine's Dock, by Tower Bridge, prompted by a desire for more space and a house on the water. The view from her window is no longer of period London, but of a less permanent, transient society of boats, pleasure steamers and barges. Seagulls circle, scavenging for food, there is a smell of salt and adventure in the air, and a new chapter begins.

Diane's new home is a modern copy of a Nash terrace, which is being transformed into her current favourite period—nineteenth-century French. Outside, it is dwarfed by glass skyscrapers and modern architecture, but the interior will reflect a fantasy world of Diane's creating. She finds a certain peace in her inaccessibility, far from the social scene of the King's Road. With new restaurants and shops to explore, and the Sunday market in Petticoat Lane, the atmosphere of this riverside oasis is reminiscent of SoHo in New York in the late 1980s.

Antique dealer **Keith Skeel** also changes homes regularly. Currently residing in a small, cosy terraced house above one of his shops in Islington, Keith is the owner of seventeen houses at the last count and is in the process of acquiring another. "At particular points in one's life there is a need to move on", he says. "A move is prompted by a combination of influences and one must be receptive to change. One can't hold onto life as if it were a photograph, encapsulated and framed forever." Keith bought this Georgian terraced house in the mid 1990s. It was envisaged as a "transit home", located conveniently above

The pink toile of the bedroom is used again for the ornate canopy above the Victorian bath (right), while the femininity of this room is emphasised by the white painted and gilt mirror above a marble hand basin to the left of the bath (bottom left). No romantic bedroom should be without a fire and a pretty mantelpiece on which to display collections of ceramics or to perch vases filled with flowers (top left).

A large collection of framed judges, acquired from a firm of lawyers in the Temple, lines both walls of Keith Skeel's narrow hallway (above).

his shop and containing certain amenities which his last London home did not have. A man who is carried by the spontaneity of the moment, Keith's mood is reflected in his surroundings. Each of his houses, dotted around the world, from London and Suffolk, to New York and Cape Town, is quite different in feel, a little imperfect, and never quite finished.

Islington has been a favourite part of London for Keith since he first decided to live here some twenty years ago. He was attracted by its proximity to Soho and London's heartland, the social accessibility of its residents, the earthy quality of Chapel Street market and the informal beauty of the Georgian squares. Everything is healthily jumbled together and, whether intentionally or not, there is no smart side

of the track, but a modern-day mix of young professionals and third-generation locals. Although Keith has never spent an entire winter in London, his house above the shop is designed for winter evenings. Purposefully painted in dark colours, with heavy curtains and blinds against the windows, each room is dominated by a large fireplace, with ornate mirrors as focal points, and corners lit by candles. His home is a curious mixture of religious symbols, from a cardinal in silk robes to a black Madonna covered in beads. There are Russian icons and saints made out of primitive papier mâché scattered among other religious objects. A collection of "framed" judges, which he got very cheaply from a lawyer's office in the Temple, has recently introduced a more severe, heavy-duty atmosphere to the entrance hall and narrow flight of stairs.

Houses are all about comfort and Keith Skeel is someone who needs order amidst the apparent chaos. Although he sells enough of them, he hates chests of drawers—the desired item of clothing is always at the bottom, resulting in an upturned drawer. As a result, his dressing room, which runs across the attic of the house, is equipped like a shop. Stainless steel scaffolding with glass shelving supports piles of neatly ironed shirts, while trousers and jackets hang in orderly rows—everything is on display. Immediately below is the bathroom, the other comfort area essential to Keith's well-being. Invariably one of the larger rooms of every house is given over to the bathroom. Grander in proportion than the bedroom, the black-and-white tiled

One wall of the bedroom is taken up with a heavy mahogany dresser filled with books and an array of blackamoors' heads (right).

Keith's drawing room was designed around the painting of a cardinal in silk robes which hangs against one wall, while at the other end of the room hangs a painting of a beautiful black Madonna, covered in beads (following double page).

The small, wood-panelled kitchen (right) is somewhat rustic in its decoration, despite a marble-topped work-table near the window.

Grand in its simplicity, the spacious bathroom (left) is where Keith does much of his creative thinking.

bathroom has no bath—comfort in this case is a practical shower squeezed into a corner and a coal fire on the wall. A cream-painted mirrored dresser contains neat piles of fresh towels and the walls are stacked with shelves of glass pharmacy bottles. Through the open window and over the high walls surrounding the courtyard garden, comes the cheerful chatter of children in the playground of the local school. It is a sound which Keith will always identify with this particular home. His next project he describes as a modern apartment. Modern but not minimal, one understands. Keith Skeel is too much of a hoarder to change his ways now.

Today, to be eligible for accommodation in Albany at the heart of Piccadilly, you simply need a lot of money. At one time, however, in the spirit of a gentlemen's club, a good character was also required. Naturally, there is a waiting list, but by the time the opportunity has presented itself, those at the top of the list have often either died or gone off to live elsewhere.

Albany was built originally in 1770–74 for first Viscount Melbourne to the design of Sir William Chambers and was known as Melbourne House. Sold to a young builder at the turn of the nineteenth century, it was converted into chambers for bachelor gentlemen, effectively the first purpose-built apartments in London. Two large blocks were added at the back on each side of the garden, separated by a covered walk-way, known as the Rope Walk, which ran from Vigo Street to Piccadilly. These were designed for gentlemen who did not want a grand establishment in London, but sought to live within easy distance of Westminster

A courtyard garden at the back links the house and the adjoining shop (top right). A riot of raised flower beds spills over with greenery, statues, urns and obelisks. A row of rusting watering cans (bottom right), each one numbered, sits lopsidedly on the garden wall and, in another corner, lines of tiny terracotta flowerpots are stacked in seed boxes giving the impression of an abacus (bottom left).

Christopher Gibbs's drawing room in Albany (right) is an eclectic mixture: a long Indian sofa with hand-painted covers and piles of Moroccan cushions, a drum from Tangiers transformed into a coffee table and an elephant's foot used as a stool. Mahogany bookshelves full of well-thumbed volumes line the walls, while the carpet, like many of his possessions, was acquired at a house sale.

and the Thames. Ladies, not originally accepted in Albany, are welcome today—not just as spouses, but as women in their own right. According to a former secretary, there was once even a dog in residence.

Christopher Gibbs, started in Albany with an attic room and moved to the rather more spacious lower floors in the mid-1970s. The layout of each of the apartments along the Rope Walk in Albany is more or less the same, with a few permutations. In the main, they comprise a drawing room leading into a bedroom, with double doors separating the two and a fireplace at the end of each room. For Christopher, one of London's best-known antique dealers, the location is ideal with St James's on the one side and Soho on the other. The luxury of such big old houses with exits into several

quarters of the town has always appealed to him. When he moved into his present apartment, he wanted it to be in harmony with the epoch that Albany was created—the first two decades of the nineteenth century. Yet he also wanted it to be comfortable, to feel as if it might be a corner of some great big country house. The rooms are elegantly designed with generous proportions. The drawing room is lined with books and carefully chosen furniture and memorabilia. He also retains an attic room, originally for servants. Here it is possible to have someone to stay in relative comfort; the writer Bruce Chatwin was an almost permanent guest for nearly five years. Since then the attic room is kept rather Spartan so that guests don't feel inclined to stay long. The bathroom is down the end of a

The original fireplace was discovered by Christopher in the cellar and reinstated. Its mantelpiece is now filled with memorabilia, engravings, photographs and cards (right).

chilly stone corridor and nowadays only a few of Christopher's toughest country friends are prepared to put up with the refined discomfort.

Christopher's love of London began in his twenties. He would spend the weekends exploring by every means—taking the bus to Hampton Court, going down-river to Greenwich, or staying up all night and walking home through the dawn. He would gaze up at the lighted windows into rooms with sensational painted ceilings or intricate plasterwork. There was a surprise around every corner. Older now, he is no less romantic and even though he knows London quite well, Christopher acknowledges that it is only well enough to realise that he hardly knows the city at all. He loves old London, elegant London, funky London, sleazy London, the charm of suburbia and its little lost villages. Arriving early for dinner in Hammersmith one evening recently, he went for a walk and came upon a tiny gothic castle sandwiched between rows of ordinary houses. There are still such amazing buildings to stumble across and it is this element of surprise that keeps Christopher enthralled.

At the foot of the brass bed in the adjoining bedroom, stands a leopard—a trophy which Christopher brought back one Christmas Eve after a desperate last-minute shopping spree. As in the drawing room, bits of antiquity mingle with family mementoes. There is a "whiff of an undergraduate's room in the holidays" about it (left and far right).

THE VICTORIAN PERIOD (1837–1901)

Albany may well have been the forerunner of the purpose-built block but there are many other period buildings, perhaps less exclusive, which follow the same basic principle. A wooden board immediately inside the front entrance to this apartment block, lists the floor on which each of the residents is located. Reminiscent of a school fixtures list, the names are outlined in faded gold lettering.

Min Hogg, editor of the magazine *The World of Interiors,* and a continuing force and inspiration behind the cult of English interior design, lives on the top floor of this late nineteenth-century building. An elderly lift with heavy metal doors, whose concertina effect more often than not catches the unaware and their belongings in a vice-like grip, heads creakingly skywards. Located in a beautiful square of late Victorian houses, Min's apartment looks down from its lofty position across the neighbouring rooftops to the domes and architectural elegance of its surroundings.

The drawing room and bedroom face east, and even on this pale and unimpressive, typically grey London morning, they are washed in a soft evocative light. In both these main rooms, every available surface—whether floor or furniture—is packed with objects.

A wonderful, orderly clutter, precious and sentimental is the result of years of collecting and accumulating. For lack of space, a clutch of pink enamel jugs

and containers in descending sizes are relegated to the floor beneath a mahogany side table. They are destined to go at some point, and have been for a while, but Min just loves her junk. Then there are the books, bursting out of every cupboard, forming untidy piles around the furniture, invading her home, slowly but surely.

As much as Min loves this space, there is simply too little of it to accommodate all of her things. She has hoarded possessions since the days when she was a student; everything has a necessary place in the scheme of things and nothing can be disposed of.

Twenty-five years ago Min left her flat in Soho for this Victorian apartment. She has always lived in the centre of things, for the heart of any city is where she feels most at home. For her, to be at the centre is like being at the controls; the noise of traffic and the bustle of passers-by are prerequi-

A long nineteenth-century sofa, upholstered in a blue and white striped Turkish awning fabric, lines one wall of the drawing room (bottom right). Min Hogg had always wanted one huge picture to hang above it and found the solution in a set of colourful varnished prints of the Burma wars which, hung together, resemble an old master. The disused fireplace (above) proves a useful hiding place for a mask and a pair of oval stones.

At the opposite end of the drawing room (right), a small circular table against a gilt-framed mirror can be transformed for dinner parties, but the clock is set permanently for lunch time!

sites for urban dwelling. Min prefers to share these necessities from high above the street, where her vantage point affords her a voyeuristic sense of involvement with her fellow Londoners.

From her kitchen window, she can look down on the tiers of roof terraces, each with neat table and chairs or an occasional sunbed, tidy rows of terracotta pots and orderly planting, in the safe knowledge that she in return cannot be spied upon. Sometimes in the summer, however, the roles are reversed. On balmy evenings she may choose to have dinner in the garden— a communal square to which all residents have access. Table and chairs, fine linen, plates, cutlery and candles will be carried down to the garden, where Min, her mother and their friends will enjoy the tranquility of their urban idyll.

Perhaps malcontent with her place among the clutter, the silhouette of a grumpy lady hangs down across an overflowing bookcase. Min has compensated for the small scale of the fireplace, made of a Derbyshire stone, by hanging a large painting of Broadstairs, Kingsgate Castle above it, and filling the mantelpiece with a mixture of English lustreware and Wedgewood basalt (right).

A walnut chest of drawers (left), its marble top crowded with objects, stands between the two windows in the drawing room.

CARNATIONS

by John Stefanidis

The chest of drawers by the bedside (left) made of geometrically inlaid chips of wood, is topped by a matching piece Min found much later for twice the price!

Old and new witches' balls hang like a bunch of untidy grapes above the bed (above) while a group of blue and white china vases huddle on the narrow mantelpiece (top left).

This *trompe l'oeil* stool was designed by Loelia Lindsay, one of the Duchesses of Westminster (bottom left).

Christophe Gollut came to college in London from his native Switzerland in 1969 and has stayed ever since. From the comfort of his huge first-floor Victorian apartment he cannot imagine anywhere else in the world he would rather live. "London is made for the slightly 'apatride', sufficiently international that there is a social group for everybody and a city where foreigners don't have to relate to the English way of life if they are not interested. London lets you live the way you want to live. You can go out every night of the week or you can cut society out altogether. Nobody seems to mind. In other big cities, if you disappear for a couple of weeks people assume you have died and cross you out of their address books without a second thought."

Christophe's Kensington apartment looks out over a communal garden to which each resident has a key. In the summer, he feels as if he is in the country, the front of his apartment concealed by the leafy branches of the tall plane trees, which line so many of London's residential streets. From his bedroom window he is overwhelmed by the scent of lilac wafting in from the garden behind. There is green in every direction. Unlike many cities, London properties usually have at least one quiet side opening onto a garden or tranquil courtyard.

Christophe is a decorator who puts rooms together with no nod to the fashion trends of the day. His style has remained more or less the same since the 1970s. An uncontrived subtlety, which gives the impression that the room has always looked that way, is combined with an effortless spontaneity, prompted by the architectural strengths and weaknesses of the property. This innate sense of style and design throws into chaos the general assumption that it is the English who have the lion's share of style. To foreigners, Christophe represents everything that is essentially English, yet to the English themselves, and among them many of his friends, he could not be more foreign!

The spacious drawing room is filled with elegantly faded Victorian furniture. Sofa and chairs come to life with colourful cushions, while fabrics from Poland and Turkey are draped over doors and the arms of chairs. Textiles and colour have always played an important part in Christophe's life, inasmuch as the architectural style and

Christophe Gollut enjoys a rare moment of inactivity in a sunlit corner of his drawing room (left). The elegantly faded furniture and variety of textiles, the portraits and "fake Canaletto" beside the fireplace, together with the casual way in which the drawing room has been put together, belie the subtlety of style which is Christophe's stock in trade.

On one side of the large
mahogany cabinet in the drawing
room (above), a French tapestry
door propped up against the
wall has a mirror behind it,
giving the impression of another
room beyond.

The "back parlour" (far right)
is decorated "à la Oscar Wilde",
dark and intimate yet comfortably,
even opulently furnished.
Opposite the grand gilt mirror is a
secret, tiny kitchen, with an oven,
hobb and small sink built into a
tall cupboard, disguised behind
the same striped wall covering.

The wardrobe, like most furniture in the apartment, struggles to contain its belongings. Christophe's "social-climbing ladder" leans casually next to it (left).

There is an ordered chaos in the bedroom (right), the blue-and-white striped walls and *trompe l'oeil* ceiling lending the room an air of impermanence, as if it were a tent ready to be packed away at a moment's notice.

the quality of light in London need colour to bring a room to life. For Christophe an interior must be cosy and conducive to comfort, and although he understands the concept of minimalism, it is not for him. The idea of living within a room decorated in graded shades of white, uncluttered and disciplined would, for him, be physically impossible. Although the word clutter comes to mind, there is a slight "Swissness", a strictness tempering his madness, which insists on a tidy arrangement of things. What then will he do when his vast commode disappears to be repaired? Each drawer is stuffed full of all those really useful items only Christophe knows where to find, the overflow already spilling out over the carpet.

Books play an important part in many people's lives and the library, far from being just a room for books, is often treated with humour and affection. There are library bedrooms and even bathrooms, dining tables surrounded by wall-to-wall bookshelves, hallways of books, bookshelves on staircases or just piles of outcasts waiting to be read.

Author, **Hugo Vickers**, is inundated with books. In fact, his two-storey flat overlooking a garden square in Kensington is ruled by them. No longer limited to the library, bookshelves have taken over his dining room, while stray books are relegated to corridors and odd corners where they can be stacked out of the way. Books which have outlived their shelf life in London are sent packing to the country.

Hugo has always liked the idea of a dividing wall made up of books. Not for him, however, a door comprised of leather books with silly titles which others have gone in for. His door is hand-made from original dust jackets, many sent in by publishers as proof copies for review, or by sympathetic friends.

The books which qualify to occupy a place in the library are meticulously arranged by date of publication. Hugo revels in strange juxtapositions—Norman Tebbitt's book next to that by Sarah Keays (who sued him for defamation). He treats books like personalities, putting sets together which, as people, would not get on. Rearranging can take all morning, since it is never simply a question of finding a new home for just one volume.

If he is researching a new project, Hugo spends time in some of the great reference libraries in London. His favourite library, and that of many other Londoners, is The London Library. Founded by Thomas Carlyle in 1841 as a subscription library to serve the needs of scholars by lending books for use at home, today it is more like a private club. With more than one million volumes, it is the largest independent lending library in the world.

Frances Partridge is the last surviving member of the Bloomsbury Set, a circle of writers and intellectuals who profoundly influenced the century with their criticism of Victorian life and values and with their own liberal morals. Influenced by the philosopher, G. E. Moore, the group of friends, many of them from Cambridge, began to meet in about 1905 at a house in Gordon Square, where they aired their ideas. Born in nearby Bedford Square, Frances

Royal biographer Hugo Vickers stands in the doorway of his apartment which separates the library from the dining room behind. He has always liked the idea of being able to walk through a wall of books, and the bookshelves to house his enormous collection—together with the secret book-lined doors—are the result.

Nicky Loutit

The fireplace in Frances Partridge's apartment (left) is occupied by Boris Anrep's well-known mosaic of a fat black cat enjoying the warmth of a permanently burning fire. Above the mantelpiece hangs a still life by Duncan Grant.

Partridge became involved with the Bloomsbury Set in the 1920s after she left Cambridge. At the time she was working in an antique book shop and, although the artist Duncan Grant had a reasonable following, the others had yet to make their mark. It was a fascinating time of social experimentation for the group, which came together as an extended family, living in conscious revolt against artistic, sexual and social conventions.

As old as the century, Frances Partridge moved to Belgravia from the country following the death of her husband, Ralph, in 1961. She has lived in the same street ever since, albeit in three different apartments. Her present drawing room, situated in a small apartment on the first floor of a row of Victorian stucco houses, has tall French windows opening onto a small roof terrace, where she likes to sit out on rare sunny days. The walls are of rose, the woodwork mustard, a colour combination that Frances has carried with her from one apartment to the next. At a desk near the window, Frances is currently working on the proofs of her latest edition of diaries. Two imposing wing-backed armchairs in loose covers of a pale pink crowd the central fireplace. The grate is concealed behind a mosaic by Boris Anrep, featuring a black cat seated before a roaring fire, and Frances is very pleased to have it back. It had been away on loan to a museum for some considerable time. "People walk all over him, Boris, that is," Frances explains. "His work can be found on the steps and landing in the National Gallery, in the Bank of England and also the Roman Catholic Cathedral." The famous portrait of Lytton Strachey by Isadora Carrington hangs in one corner of the room, while a drawing of Frances's daughter by Vanessa Bell is at one end of a long bookcase. A still life by Duncan Grant and a painting entitled *The Mystery Man of Bloomsbury,* by Henry Lamb, hang over the spot where Frances is working. The bookcases that line two walls of the room carry complete works by Lytton Strachey and Virginia Woolf, while Frances Partridge's own work, takes up considerable space on one of the lower shelves.

According to Frances, London has changed beyond all recognition in the last

Numerous treasures are harboured in this Bloomsbury apartment, such as the famous portrait of Lytton Strachey by Isadora Carrington (above) or one of many photograph albums on a nearby bookshelf (below).

forty years. It has lost its uniformity and a good deal of its elegance. For her, only towns like Bath, which were built all at once, seem to have survived well.

Chelsea is a curious mixture of tiny streets with small cottages, smart blocks of mansion flats with grand entrances, expensive streets of exclusive properties surrounded by large gardens and some of the best situated council housing in the whole of London, offering unparalleled views of the Thames.

The subculture of Chelsea, however, is still strictly Bohemian. Once a playground for the artistic set, who relied on wealthy patrons to provide food and shelter, there are still many studios and other structures reminiscent of an artistic life, hidden away in the back streets. Some are simply small mews dwarfed by towering mansion blocks, others are purpose-built and idyllically set in private grounds, to this day untouched, unmodernised and, in some cases, still used primarily as working studios.

As property prices in London have gone through the roof over the last twenty years, many struggling artists have been forced out of their studios, making way for artists of a more commercial fashion—architects, interior designers, specialist painters and the like, who seek the unusual and the unique in which to set up home.

Chelsea Studios is a small enclave of artists' studios built at the turn of the century by Manenti, an Italian sculptor. He bought up the gardens belonging to two Georgian houses fronting the Fulham Road and then designed and built some thirty studios for his wife and her friends, thus

creating a thriving and authentic artistic environment.

Over the years, artists came and went, but a core of residents stayed and a true sense of community spirit developed. Communal gardens with small lawns bordered with beds of roses and shrubs divide the rows of studios. Fountains, a small pond with huge fish, an occasional slate seat and interesting sculptures are dotted around the gardens. Protected from the hubbub of the Fulham Road by a high whitewashed wall, access is gained through two ancient studded wooden doors.

A glimpse of the sanctuary through a closing door is enough to convince most curious passers-by that a secret paradise lies within. Cats sun themselves in quiet corners and, in summer, a group of residents, known collectively as the Tea Set, do the same, moving their chairs, cups and saucers around the garden, keeping track with the sun.

Everyone knows each other but they keep their distance—that typically British combination of "hail fellow, well met", with-

Sparsely furnished to enhance the unique height of the studio, a natural sculpture of a wind-blown piece of driftwood is the sole decoration (top right). Billa, the bull-terrier and lady of the house, seems to appreciate her surroundings (above).

The north-facing skylight in the studio can be glimpsed through the translucent colours of a row of saris hanging across the entrance to the galleried bedroom (right).

A simple window, devoid of curtains, (below) frames a beautiful pomegranate tree outside whose peculiar orange flowers and small dark green leaves create a natural, living painting throughout the summer.

out the invasion of privacy which can often follow any greeting. A curt nod or brief smile is enough to know that you are part of the scene; a stranger is regarded with as much animosity as someone entering a pub full of locals—the breaking of an unwritten code.

The "Italian Village", as these studios are known, nestles against a high wall, which was once the only structure separating them from the Chelsea football ground. Paths circumnavigate the plot, doors and steep steps disappear in all directions, while motley roofs betray the television aerials of modern-day existence. No one studio resembles another. Some have been remodelled, kitchens and bathrooms introduced to the original workspace, others retain their original structure.

Living in a room designed as a workplace has its disadvantages. Many studios are not insulated and some have no central heating, so seasonal changes are felt as much inside as out—a hothouse in summer or icy cold in winter.

Dinner parties are often less than elegant, since guests can be reluctant to remove their overcoats at the table. Such artists' studios are not limited to Chelsea, however, Hampstead and Notting Hill have a liberal sprinkling, with others dotted around London.

One wonderful studio has belonged to the same family for at least two generations. Successive painters and sculptors have sought refuge here, the present occupant combining sculpture and architecture in delightful chaos. One side of the studio is taken over by a massive wooden table

A delightful chaos of art and life invades this huge Victorian artist's studio, where every inch of available floorspace is taken up by busts and statues, sacks of clay, paintings and treasured possessions.

At the other end of the studio (left) a pair of comfortable sofas is grouped around a vast brick fireplace. Stacks of books and papers have taken over the corner office, which is bathed in light from windows set high in the wall. On the edge of the mantelpiece (far right) a group of terracotta busts crowds a Victorian oil lamp.

covered with bowls of smooth pebbles, plates of exotic shells, piles of paper and drawings, stacks of books and general work in progress. Every available surface is crammed with terracotta nudes—draped, posed, embracing or sleeping. Ornate chandeliers flank a marble-topped table above which hangs a vast gilt mirror, while in the corner a marble statue of a kilt-clad Scottish youth observes the scene. The effect of this unexpectedly imposing arrangement is offset immediately by a scruffy office chair raised on boxes and used for sittings. It is surrounded by busts and assorted bags of clay, while on a nearby bench, an old engine part rests against a reclining nude.

Two ancient sofas are set at right angles to a central fireplace, where logs brought up from the country are aflame. Walls are lined with hessian and painted taupe and the mantelpiece is covered with sculpted busts and a collection of unwound French clocks. Piles of books are everywhere and a sort of office is squeezed into the far corner; the desk is littered with a sense of urgent activity while light streams in through a skylight and windows set high in the wall.

Despite the studio's mid-nineteenth-century romantic atmosphere, the antiquated and the modern hold equal fascination for the present owner. An intriguing bronze spare part from a Spitfire is a recent acquisition, the Victorian toy steam engine, on a low stool, brought to life for a child's rare visit to his father's sanctuary. Juxtaposed against this collection of engineering history, modern technology is represented in the shape of the latest fax machine at one end of the table. A projector is suspended from the high ceiling on a small platform, electric fans silently stir the air and the evocative candlelight can be boosted, at the touch of a button, by a state of the art lighting system.

Amidst the apparent chaos, there is an order and a sense of continuity. The variety of things scattered randomly about the room reflects the owner's diverse interests, from 1930s airplanes, cogs and other marvels of engineering, to a collection of his own black and white photographs tacked to one wall, books on art and catalogues from the Royal Academy. The studio is the birthplace of its owner's creativity—where projects and passions have started life. A place of inspiration, it has a monastic seclusion with no windows other than those high under the roof, no view to distract the artist's thoughts. Here he can enjoy a privacy and spiritual calm instilled by centuries of ephemera. Everything has its place and has been in it for years, waiting to be adopted into a new scheme.

THE EDWARDIAN PERIOD (1901–1910)

In another London neighbourhood, near Chelsea, the sound of young voices reverberates from the red-brick buildings surrounding a smooth macadam courtyard: a small crowd of children has gathered around a stray supermarket trolley and they are giving each other rides. The smallest and most vocal child has succeeded in attaining the status of permanent co-pilot as the trolley is swung round and round the yard. The more raucous cries of the game drift in through the open windows of the flat at the far end of the courtyard. Situated up several flights of cold cement stairs, forever associated with the smell of strong disinfectant and new paint, the door on this particular landing stands out. It has a particularly smart knocker in the shape of a delicate hand.

The Samuel Lewis Buildings, consisting of austere housing blocks, were created in 1910 for "the artisan and labouring poor of London" in order to provide rentable accommodation to those who had jobs and were not dependent on the state. Families have lived here for successive generations. It is a microcosm of real life, more all-consuming than the most imaginative television soap opera. Everyone knows their neighbours' business and the latest scandal is inevitably the main topic of conversation. Families intermarry and move into the block across the yard and the gossip continues.

Joan Hecktermann's drawing room shares space with a dining table and assorted chairs which, on the rare occasion when Joan is not entertaining, are pushed back against a wall of books and personal treasures (below).

A large sofa bed is concealed under a loose cover of cream linen, the door into the narrow hall held permanently open by a glass-fronted cabinet filled with bones, skulls and coral (right).

J oan has turned an austere housing block apartment into an exotic mix of souvenirs from her childhood in Kenya and the streets of modern London. A lampshade made of porcupine quills perches on the narrow window sill (left).

A set of large femurs rests beneath an eclectic collection of pictures, photographs and drawings (above).

The apartment of **Joan Hecktermann,** which waits behind a door adorned with the unusually elegant knocker, would probably surprise most of its neighbours not so much by its simplicity as by its non-conformity. Painted white throughout and furnished with a minimum of fuss and pretension, one enters a narrow corridor leading straight into a light and airy drawing room. A lifetime of trips abroad is recounted here: bleached bones of every size and description are ranked alongside a vase of Arum lilies, a collection of smooth pebbles, feathers, a piece of sinuous wood. Many were gifts and each has a place earmarked on the shelf, its position in the hierarchy of sentimental objects.

Joan Hecktermann is currently housesitting for a friend. She arrived one day with two suitcases: one filled with old bones and the memorabilia of a happy childhood in Kenya, the other with the rubbish necessary for living in a city.

After attending art college in Chelsea, Joan has lived in the area on and off ever since. Early on she shared with the family of a wealthy friend in Kensington Court, then spent several years as a sitting tenant in a huge flat on the Cromwell Road. The only residents of the entire building, Joan and a friend became famous for their "stair parties" held on the vast marble staircase that ran the height of the house. With no neighbours to disturb and little rent to pay, this dream lasted a good while. Her present eyrie is an ideal stop-gap, located just a stone's throw from the Michelin Building and a host of smart designer boutiques.

Walking out of the door at weekends, however, can be somewhat daunting—dressed in paint-bespattered clothing, Joan often has to pass the Joseph boutique on the way to the supermarket for a pint of milk. The plethora of trim "ladies who lunch" dressed in ubiquitous beige and black can be very intimidating and she often scuttles back thankfully behind the enclosing walls of the mansion blocks to lose herself in their austere anonymity.

Yet she finds that this juxtaposition of cheap housing with some of London's most expensive and trendy boutiques is a pleasing balance. In the end, what Joan loves about London is the choice that it gives her between solitude and the company of others. She draws her artistic inspiration, however, not from London, but from the deserts and vast open spaces from which she comes.

The tiny kitchen, which has at times been known to feed the five thousand, is blessed with a Baby Belling in lieu of a proper oven. Joan likes the impromptu feeling of camping and the lack of kitchen gadgets. Instead of fine china, a wooden shelf (right) is packed with a series of neatly labelled boxed shells and a striking poster by Cy Twombly.

Cy Twombly
Oct 18 1980
at
Yvon
Lambert
5 Rue Du Grenier
St Lazare
UROCOPTIS
BREVIS

CONVERSIONS

To install a contemporary interior behind the façade of a Victorian or Edwardian building is a challenge taken up by a number of creative thinkers. Some architects, such a Richard Rogers and John Pawson, have even gone so far as to combine certain of their minimalist constructions with Victorian buildings.

Walton Street is located at the heart of fashionable Brompton Cross and the boutiques which satellite around the Michelin Building. A favourite haunt of many with both time and money on their hands, the street is lined with shops specialising in interior design, jewellery and fashion, intermingled with some of London's newest and coolest restaurants.

At the Harrods end of Walton Street, **Gül Coskun** has recently bought a small sliver of a house, tucked anonymously down a narrow alleyway. The front door opens onto a steep set of stairs which lead up to the first floor drawing room.

The decoration is modern, Walton Street beige and black on an uncarpeted floor. The walls are lined with a wonderful collection of screen prints by Andy Warhol. Music is playing quietly in the background, as Warhol's Mohammed Ali shakes his fist

The light and modern interior of Gül Coskun's apartment forms a perfect backdrop for an exhibition of screen prints by Andy Warhol. The drawing room (far left) is home to Liz Taylor, while the small office is dominated by Marilyn Monroe (left). This splendid head of Hercules takes advantage of a light corner in the kitchen (right).

at Lenin across the drawing room. Ingrid Bergman has taken refuge with Beethoven in the kitchen and a Picasso currently hangs as a headboard above Gül's bed under the eaves. Art on show in a domestic environment catches the imagination in a quite different way than a more formal exhibition and this subtle approach has been the mark of Gül's success. She has turned her house into the backdrop for a permanent series of exhibitions of the three artists in which she has chosen to specialise:

Matisse, Picasso and Warhol. A Sotheby's training, followed by a period with interior designer Nicholas Haslam, provided Gül with a precious combination of artistic knowledge and intuitive good taste which she has finally taken advantage of. By limiting her field, Gül has acquired a specialist knowledge and a reputation on the art circuit for putting on a good show. At Gül's place, people from the music industry and the fashion world mingle with bankers and other young professionals, united by a curiosity or a passion for Andy Warhol. Gül likens her exhibitions to the "salons" of former times, where strangers can meet in a convivial atmosphere and disperse into quiet corners of the house to converse.

As exhibitions change, and the focus of attention swings from Warhol to Matisse, so the decoration of Gül's house changes, chameleon-like, to fit the new mood. For Matisse, a Moroccan ambience with lanterns, chair covers, a new layout in the drawing room and carpets on the normally bare floors. A soft African drumming sets the tone. Small cups of strong coffee are served in the kitchen and the wall colouring of the entrance hall now evokes something Saharan.

Living in a permanent gallery demands a certain discipline. The same can be said for a barely furnished house in London, although in addition to a minimalist constraint, a really good central heating system is a necessity.

For designer **Clare Lloyd,** converting a classic Victorian stucco-fronted property with numerous standard-sized rooms, wasteful passages and unusable spaces, into

a free-flowing, minimalist interior took imagination and a gritty determination to get things done. Clare's life, however, has not always been ruled by an austere outlook. When she arrived in London from Sydney in 1983, she lived in a minute flat in Fulham, barely eight-feet wide. At the time, Clare found Londoners closed and disinterested, while the pace of the city made it difficult for her to establish an identity. Her reaction to this solitude was to fill her space with objects. As her life changed, so did her home. She cleared out the furniture and painted everything white. Many possessions went into storage and the first tentative steps towards a minimalist lifestyle were taken.

Australians are always associated with Earl's Court, at the edge of Chelsea, known derogatorily by the locals as "Kangaroo Valley", since this is where all newly-arrived back-packers seem to gravitate when first setting foot in London. Although the area of red-brick mansion blocks and garden squares is still Clare's favourite part of London, associated with some of the hap-

G lossy black-painted floorboards and the occasional linen-clad armchair enhance the monochrome minimalism of Clare Lloyd's house in Notting Hill (left).

R esting on a solid plinth, an immense table made of poured cement mixed with granite powder, dominates the dining room (above).

piest periods of her life, she finally chose to settle down in Notting Hill.

Her first introduction to the area was on a photo shoot at the house which is located literally opposite the one she eventually would buy. Clare fell in love with the street, intoxicated by the light and the

The basement is given over to monumental elements in the kitchen and dining room (above), united by a smooth, off-white concrete floor. The overall uniformity is cut by a flight of black-painted stairs at the far side.

sense of well-being which she felt. Notting Hill radiated an air of excitement and had a younger, more adventurous streak than the more established, familiar squares of Chelsea.

The result of many months of careful planning, hard work and endless construc-

tion nightmares is a house with an extraordinary sense of space and light. All the walls of one floor were torn down to create a drawing room stretching the length of the house. The scant furniture is united by a monochrome colour scheme of black-painted floorboards and off-white walls, with natural linen covering sofa and chairs. There are two simple fireplaces—no side tables, no bric-a-brac, no extraneous clutter.

Descend to garden level and the high-ceilinged basement is dominated by a dining table of poured cement mixed with granite powder, resting on a solid plinth. A cement floor unites the dining room with the kitchen, where a hob, oven and kitchen sink have been sunk into another huge block. Everything is a natural and purely simple off-white colour. The smooth concrete floor extends out through the French windows to form a small courtyard garden, with flower beds and large terracotta pots containing meticulously-clipped bay trees placed strategically along the garden's back edge.

With this move, Clare has refined, rather than changed her style—the differences are expressed in proportion and the quality of light. Her new house, however, exerts greater architectural influence and discipline and it was almost easier, despite its size, to house her paintings and furniture in her former little flat. In Notting Hill, she has had to pare down her belongings even further, keeping only those few items which really work.

Continuing the monochrome theme, the L-shaped bedroom is light, spacious and uncluttered. Clothing and other banished items are relegated to a row of seamless cupboards (right).

MODERN INTERIORS

One corner of the drawing room of Sir Terence Conran's penthouse apartment is given over to a towering sculpture of empty cigar boxes, a photograph of Eileen Gray by Beresford and three sticks by Antonio Carluccio (top right).

Eduardo Paolozzi created the maquette of a head (below), the original of which stands outside the Design Museum.

A desire for space and an uncluttered existence popularised living in London's Docklands in the 1980s. Warehouse conversions offered a new alternative to the cramped flats and traditional houses available in other parts of the city.

Spearheaded by **Sir Terence Conran**, the conversion of the dimly lit, foggy streets around Butler's Wharf into a community of offices and apartments—serviced with local shops, restaurants and bars—heralded a promising future for the neglected and, in many cases, derelict Victorian warehouses which lined both banks of the Thames east of Tower Bridge.

Unfortunately, these grand reminders of England's days of trading supremacy were not always treated with the respect they deserved. Only a few of the great brick ware-

houses were converted with any imagination or sensitivity, the rest falling victim to property developers with little sense of their history.

Forty years ago, London was still very much a working port city, with barges and ships going right up the river. At the time, Lord Snowdon was working on a book, *London, 1959*. He had taken a room in Rotherhithe and remembers, with an overwhelming sense of nostalgia, the fog horns on the Thames at night, and the noise of the metal barges knocking against each other in the wake of a passing ship outside his window.

The fog was sometimes so thick that it could be cut with a knife. It was a romantic time, in the true sense of the word. Sometimes, at low tide, Snowdon would climb out of his window onto the beach and walk to the local pub, The Mayflower. Until recently it was the only pub in London where one could buy stamps, being the last port of call for boats leaving for the continent.

Three walls of windows make for a luminous drawing room. The chaise longue is by Marcel Breuer and the resin chair by Karuselli. The remaining furnishings, as one would expect, are mainly pieces of Conran's own design, among them the sofas and central coffee table.

The ornate metal table in the entrance hall (following double page) was discovered in several pieces in Isle-sur-la-Sorgue in the region of Vaucluse, France. It is now used to display a collection of glassware, both antique and new.

Back then, even before Conran, Lord Snowdon had entertained grand plans for the river. His idea was to install lock gates below Tower Bridge and make the Thames non-tidal, leaving the area around St Paul's cathedral free of buildings, and redeveloping the South Bank for residents of every income.

While Snowdon's project never got off the ground, after twenty years in the making, Conran's Docklands dream has still to reach fruition. It seems to be an area of promise, destined never to be fulfilled.

Nevertheless, Conran has achieved success with a more personal project. In the words of William Morris, "the house that would please me would be some great room where one talked to one's friends in one corner and ate in another and slept in another and worked in another."

Terence Conran has turned those words into a reality. "If people want large spaces, they can make their own. New architecture gives people the opportunity of organising their space for the way they really live."

Recently, he and his girlfriend, Vicky Davis, moved into the two-storey penthouse above Conran's offices. It is like living in a glass house, the interior drenched in light at all times of the day. It was their first real attempt at modern living. Conran had spent his life in Georgian buildings, trying to adapt them to a modern way of life. Life on the river does have its drawbacks, for example, an acceptable neighbourhood noise level is amplified by water, the surrounding tall brick buildings acting like loudspeakers.

Yet, with a house in the country as a safety net and a diary that would make most people reach for the tranquillisers, the penthouse above the shop has proved a godsend. In the evenings, when the builders have gone home and the dust has settled, it is extraordinarily peaceful.

In Clerkenwell, an area just north of the City which has recently enjoyed a resurgence of investment, old factories and warehouses are being converted, restaurants and art galleries are opening up, and the music industry is taking over previously empty office space. A former printing factory is being turned into, quite literally, cubes of space for the daring and enlightened to call home.

Into this scene, enter a couple who have spent their entire married life in a traditional Victorian house in Essex, on the outskirts of London. At a time when **Paul Vaight** is thinking of retiring, he and his wife Sue have bought a cube, 2,500 square feet to be exact, with floor to ceiling windows and a wonderful sense of space. Now the family live in London on weekends and spend weekdays in the country.

With the help of Circus Architects, it took six months of family collaboration to transform the concrete cell. Where architects tend to concentrate on space and shape, the Vaights came up with ideas for colour. Apricot ceilings, originally treated as a joke, are now a feature of the final design. Moving to Clerkenwell, the family has had to re-invent itself. Furniture and other belongings are now scattered around the houses of Rochester after a large sale in the garden of their former home. The

Awash with light from above, the kitchen opens onto a plant-filled conservatory (left). Integrated into the overall open plan of the penthouse, the centrepiece of the kitchen is a Conran-designed central wooden table with stools from Butler's Wharf Chop House Restaurant created by Conran near Tower Bridge.

The daily papers are rolled tightly and stored in a basket, ready for lighting the drawing-room stove.

The rigid lines of the Paul Vaight's Clerkenwell cube are offset by the curved walls of the entrance hall (right).

discipline of a modern loft banishes all ideas of clutter. The sense of space is maintained by the sculptural quality of the colourful furniture—newly acquired and wholly appropriate—and the minimalist kitchen.

Location in London has always been important. Where one lives is as vital as how one lives. Yet, there are distinct advantages to living in an area of London which has no identity. There can be no stereotypical reactions, no snobbish comments. Creative

types, whether artists, sculptors or photographers, seem drawn to buildings not originally designed for habitation and which, for this very reason, are located off the beaten track in areas which are considered by most to be unfashionable. Thus, factories and empty warehouses in the East End, for example, have been gradually taken over by an artistic community, galleries have appeared to take advantage of the new talent and a regeneration of entire streets is the end result. This is not a new trend. In

Unusual apricot ceilings in the large open-plan living space (right), combine with the deep, bright shades of modern furniture to create a truly unique environment.

A metal staircase (right), reminiscent of a ship's gangplank, leads up to the mezzanine floor (left), with its comfortable sitting area.

the days when Chelsea was a struggling village, it was the artists who moved in and popularised the area, attracting the interest of more demanding residents once they had created a Bohemian environment.

For **Simon Upton,** who had spent his childhood on the Welsh borders, the appeal of taking up residence on the edge of relatively uncharted territory and in a shell of a building which he could design entirely to suit himself, seems quite natural. Initially, it was intended as a working studio; the need for somewhere to live as well seemed a minor detail at the time. Intent on using the proportions of the huge room to the best advantage, at one end he installed a modern stainless steel kitchen unit, the only permanent fixture in the place. A bathroom, concealed behind a wall of glass bricks, and a small guest room opposite, have restored a symmetrical balance to the main space. Next he established a sitting, thinking and drawing area in the

In Simon Upton's studio every object evokes a voyage. Indonesian "life" cloths hang from the glass-fronted gallery (right), zebra skins are stretched out on the wooden floor, a Kuba cloth hangs above a French seamstress's table (left), while lion and ram skulls and glasses filled with porcupine quills decorate spare surfaces (below).

middle, made all the more conducive by the introduction of a pair of comfortable sofas. They divide the room up rather conveniently and form a visual break where the stairs descend from the gallery bedroom.

A lover of the classical period, Simon's studio has a modern interpretation: its simple design, symmetrical and with conscious form, is echoed in the interior layout and the careful placing of the furniture. There are no corners to fill, so the design remains uncluttered.

Painted an all-over white, the choice of colour for the studio was not Simon's first option. Guided by the initial impulse to use his studio as a workplace, any tendency towards colour was deliberately curbed, prompted by concern at the cast it might throw. White walls, white upholstery, even

The small dressing room is decorated with etchings from the Middle and Far East by Charles Cain and a Grazalema rug from Andalusia lies folded on the makeshift bed.

When Simon goes away, as he frequently does, nothing will have changed on his return. There are no plants to wilt from lack of attention, the porcupine quills, old bones, skulls and ostrich eggs will all be there when he gets back.

His dream of a nomadic existence is acted out in the bedroom, where a central bed on the gallery is draped in a natural linen closely resembling a tent. Animal skins cover the floor and bright textiles are thrown over an old leather armchair. Cocooned with the more precious of his belongings, he is free to become a mind-traveller. London is temporarily blanked out behind opaque blinds, while he revisits the places he has passed through so rapidly, dwelling on those areas with which he identified most strongly.

City life can be a stressful existence, a daily battle to maintain one's individuality against a tide of conformity. One's home offers stability and protection from the world outside the window, and the way in which each living space is decorated and furnished reinforces that fragile sense of identity. The cultural variety of London's residents is reflected in their homes. The wide use of colour and textiles, the fascinating accumulation of objects and mementoes from far-flung places, together with a certain British style is evident. One glance around a room reveals more about the personality of the owner than any casual conversation. If the exteriors of some of London's streets appear to lack variety, no two interiors will look alike—the individual interpretation of each space affording an intriguing insight into the lives of others.

a white floor, may seem a touch over-disciplined, but the result is aesthetically very pleasing.

Travellers are normally obsessed with the phantom of permanency and the psychological burden of possessions, yet the eclectic collection of furniture and objects strategically placed around the studio would seem to prove that this traveller is an exception to the rule. The architecturally classic and simple space has become an ideal backdrop for the very personal mixture of furniture, its symmetry ensuring that everything can be moved around at will, without upsetting the balance. A dark Jacobean armoire sits easily within the open-plan room, juxtaposed with a modern dining table and an uneven number of beautifully sculpted Art Nouveau chairs. The coffee table separating the two white sofas is made of cardboard boxes, simply joined together with black gaffer tape.

The four-poster bed on the gallery (right) is made of Patuk wood from India and is tented with a natural linen.

A wall of glass bricks divides the white bathroom (left) from the modern kitchen located at the far end of the open-plan loft (far left).

The back of the white sofa is draped with a mud cloth from Mali, while a round table at the entrance to the loft bears a cowhide basket and other travel trophies.

A MAN'S WORLD

NEW & LINGWOOD

Jermyn Street in St James's is lined with shops selling everything from gentlemen's shirts to accessories. One of the more famous names is that of New & Lingwood where gentlemen have their shirts made-to-measure (right).

Reels of brightly coloured cotton thread line the yellow mantelpiece in the reception room of bespoke tailor Timothy Everest's Spitalfields house (preceding double page).

For some two hundred years, since the time of Beau Brummell's emergence as the arbiter of male elegance, England—and London in particular—has never stopped attracting dandies and well-dressed gentlemen. In a world where tradition, quality and service are still valued above all things, the English "look" is greatly prized and universally copied.

The very heart of men's fashion can be found in St James's, where time seems to have stood still. Here, gentlemen may have their shoes, shirts and suits made-to-measure. They buy their cases of vintage port, their cigars, their hats and umbrellas in exclusive shops, many of which have been open for a century or two. They lunch in traditional restaurants or meet discreetly in their private clubs. A subtle atmosphere of tradition reigns, an art of gracious living.

It is true that Englishmen—of a certain social class, of course—have always shown an interest in their clothes and in the art of dressing. Today, while mass production has succeeded in sublimating any individuality in style or dress in most of the western world, there has been a major revival in the tailoring industry in England.

It is certainly time for such a revival. The tradition epitomised by Savile Row has dwindled to a limited number of professionals. Although there has always been a core clientele of English gentlemen, British tailoring skills are more often sold abroad to Japanese and American connoisseurs, who appreciate the English art of dressing and are quite happy to pay for the luxury. This art of dressing is wonderfully exemplified in English period dramas and Hollywood films—as seen in the sartorial elegance of James Mason or David Niven.

Even today, you can still catch the occasional glimpse of a beautifully tailored back, or the flash of an exotic silk lining on the streets of London. For example, a tall, slim figure in a large-scale check suit with an unusually long jacket steps out of a doorway in Savile Row in London's West End. He is one of this new generation of young professionals starting to take an interest in the art of dressing. The suit is designed by Richard James, the only member of the "new" Savile Row who is actually based on the famous street itself.

THE "SAVILE ROW" SPIRIT

British tailors are re-inventing themselves. While the traditional firms continue to cater for an older, more conservative clientele, a new generation of tailors has spread around the West End. One, perhaps more daring and confident than the others, has moved his office as far away as possible

Madonna adores tailor Richard James (opposite) who also numbers Christian Lacroix among his clients. His shop is in Savile Row, where gentlemen's tailors have been located since the nineteenth century.

Timothy Everest has chosen to decorate the interior of his Georgian premises in Elder Street in historical colours, the green tone of the wood panelling in the main hallway and staircase (left) providing a perfect background for the selection of brightly coloured silk ties (right) displayed on the first floor landing. The waxed yellow of the front parlour, which is used as a reception room, has the atmosphere of a gentleman's club, the door used to advantage to show off the designs of a few more ties (below).

The façade of the Royal Academy on Piccadilly is reflected in the windows of Fortnum & Mason, probably London's most famous gourmet food store (below) and located in the heart of the exclusive shopping district of St James's and Mayfair.

from the accepted centre of bespoke tailors. Tim Everest, in fact, has established himself at the other end of the rag-trade spectrum, amongst the houses of the former Huguenot silk weavers in Spitalfields in London's East End.

Tim is trying to demystify the custom-tailored garment by providing an updated interpretation of the quintessential Englishman's style of dress. Yet, if his intention is to make bespoke tailoring more accessible, his geographical choice of location could not be less so. The narrow townhouse on Elder Street, a stone's throw from the financial hub of London, was a purely romantic whim which, in retrospect, has worked well, but could just as well have proved disastrous. The historical atmosphere of Elder Street has given Tim's choice of location an air of intrigue, piquing sufficiently the curiosity of the majority of his loyal clientele to persuade them to make the journey from the West End.

The secret to a gentleman's idea of shopping would appear to be the economy of time in its achievement. Thus, tailors, bootmakers, shirtmakers and hatters steal the advantage from each other by sticking together, either occupying the same premises, or at best the same street, to capture a market with little time and even less interest in the job at hand.

Hence the luxury of bespoke shoes, where the only visit required is to fit the lasts, made exactly to the design of one's own feet, every single bump and imperfection incorporated. The purchase

London is a city for all those gentlemen who appreciate a touch of luxury. At John Lobb, the famous bootmaker (below), a bespoke pair of shoes can take several months to fashion, but are well worth the wait.

Covered passages afford Londoners the joys of shopping no matter what the weather. The famous Burlington Arcade (right) from the Regency period is the place to buy sumptuous cashmere, while the nearby Piccadilly Arcade (far right) leads to the New & Lingwood shop.

there was reputedly a time when the only woman one would meet in St James's was either a duchess or a prostitute.

Originally famous for its coffee and chocolate houses, St James's soon became popular for its clubs and shops. Time has literally stood still for some of the original shops of the period, as seen in the ancient façades of Berry Bros. & Rudd, James Lock

of a new pair of shoes, thereafter, is simply a matter of a telephone call. The same can be said of bespoke tailoring, where patterns for a variety of suits carry the secret of every detail of a man's anatomy and can be ordered with very little time wasted. It is surprising how many gentlemen are still wearing suits they had made some thirty years ago and are prodigiously proud of the fact.

St James's has always been synonymous with elegance, style and money. The area immediately surrounding St James's Palace, which became an important royal residence at the end of the seventeenth century, has since enjoyed a reputation as a fashionable place to be seen, as well as an almost exclusively male preserve. One has only to note the concentration of gentlemen's clubs in this area. Indeed,

& Co. and John Lobb, forming a trio of vintner, hatter and bespoke bootmaker at the lower end of St James's Street.

Over the years, these have been joined by other shops. Jermyn Street, which enjoyed a reputation in the early nineteenth century for good hotels, enhanced this image with a variety of shops specialising in menswear—from shirtmakers, bootmakers and hatters to those

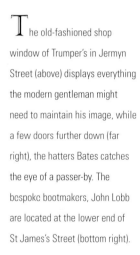

A collection of elegant canes, rustic walking sticks and umbrellas (left) displayed inside the shop of James Lock & Co., hatters, in St James's Street. Patronised by both Beau Brummell and Lord Byron in their day, this famous hatter has been located in St James's for more than two hundred years.

The old-fashioned shop window of Trumper's in Jermyn Street (above) displays everything the modern gentleman might need to maintain his image, while a few doors further down (far right), the hatters Bates catches the eye of a passer-by. The bespoke bootmakers, John Lobb are located at the lower end of St James's Street (bottom right).

providing gentlemen's accessories, such as jewellery, perfume and tobacco along with the all-important barber.

The Victorian specialist men's shops of St James's and Mayfair are still British fashion's best-kept secret. Suppliers to men of the Empire, these shops prospered through the Victorian retailing boom which peaked in 1890, offering a classic style wholly unaffected by the vagaries of fashion. Remarkably, it is this style and quality that is still in demand today and which prompts an extraordinary number of gentlemen to go to great lengths and considerable expense to dress and style themselves after the traditional fashion. Thus, the popularity of the unique bespoke services, still provided by the more than few companies that have survived down the centuries, seems guaranteed.

FOR MEMBERS ONLY

St James's Street also boasts several venerable gentlemen's clubs, which were originally described as "buildings for the exclusive use of members for generally social and entertainment purposes." In some cases, they also offer temporary residence. It was considered a great distinction to be elected a member of one of these clubs, where gentlemen could behave as they wished, not needing to observe any of the niceties of the day.

The early clubs were essentially places for dining; in the seventeenth century they took on a more distinctive character with the rise of coffee houses and their establishment in smart surroundings. The landlord of the coffee house would allocate a special room for club use at no charge, hoping to profit from both the food and drink he might sell to members, and the distinction conferred upon his premises by the presence of notable men.

The number and variety of clubs increased rapidly and their founding principles were mainly of a socio-political nature. White's, the oldest and grandest, was founded in 1693 at White's Chocolate House. Its list of members goes back over 250 years and includes some of high society's richest and most influential men, including several English monarchs and prime ministers.

By the eighteenth century, White's and the later Brooks's Club—an artistically inclined house, known as the arbiter of literary taste—had become famous for their members' obsession with gambling

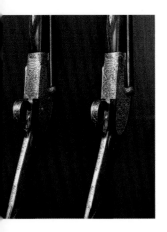

A pair of 20-bore side-locks at Purdey's in South Audley Street (above) where a gentleman can place an order for a new gun or have a prized antique repaired.

for high stakes, a reputation that continued well into the next century.

The famous Boodle's was established in 1762 on the site of the first White's premises, and boasted the Duke of Wellington and William Wilberforce among its members. It was originally called the "Scavoir Vivre" and renowned for its cuisine. Today, its members are predominantly country-based, and use the club for short forays to London. The Carlton was set up fifty years later after a general election in which the Tories lost a large number of seats and wanted a social club in which to meet. Membership was greatly sought after by many an aspiring Conservative, but it was after 1912 that the club rules indicated that those of any other political persuasion would not be welcome. Members are still required to be British subjects and supporters of the Conservative Party and nearly all former Conservative prime ministers, Winston Churchill among them, have been members at one time.

By the nineteenth century, many clubs were trying to find permanent premises, often in the form of imposing houses built for them by well-known architects. They also became more specialised; certain clubs were reserved for the military, and The Garrick was one of the earlier theatrical foundations.

At the southern end of St James's, Pall Mall, a fashionable street from its inception, gradually became the preferred location for gentlemen's clubs. Among the grand and imposing façades on this wide boulevard are the anonymous portals of the Athenaeum, the most intellectually elite of

London's clubs, founded in 1824; the Reform, established for Radicals in 1836; the Royal Automobile Club of 1897; and several other hallowed shrines of masculinity.

The Travellers' Club was founded in 1819 as a point of reunion for gentlemen who had travelled abroad. An original pre-requisite of membership was that one had to have travelled a minimum of five hundred miles outside the British Isles in a direct line from London. Designed by Charles Barry, the Travellers' Club was built in the style of an Italian palazzo. The building occupies an area adjoining the site of Carlton House, which was demolished in 1826 when George IV moved to Buckingham Palace.

Today, the old-fashioned notion of membership-only clubs has lost none of its original appeal. Mark's Club and Harry's Bar are two of the best restaurants in London, but reserved for members only, while several new restaurants, such as The Bluebird, have private dining rooms. Clubs, including The Cobden in Notting Hill, provide members with dining and music, and the majority of the nightclubs in London are not open to the general public.

In the wake of increased demand and a renewed fascination with the world of cigar smoking, 1997 saw the launch of the Cigar Club in Percy Street, the first club of its kind in London, while the Little Havana Cigar Bar in Leicester Place boasts the longest bar in London. The first Cuban cigars arrived in London in 1830 and were sold through Robert Lewis, now known as James J. Fox and Robert Lewis, the oldest

B ates (right), celebrated for its classic Panama hats, has a small shop in Jermyn Street lined from floor to ceiling with hat boxes of all shapes, sizes and dimensions.

The hallowed grounds of the gentlemen's clubs, the majority of which are located around St James's Street and Pall Mall, are one of London's best kept secrets. The classical library at The Travellers' Club (facing page) is famed for its elegance, while the Outer Morning Room (above) is often used by members for a game of chess over morning coffee or a quiet read of the day's newspapers.

tobacco merchants in England. Among their customers were two famous cigar connoisseurs: Oscar Wilde and Sir Winston Churchill.

MALE ELEGANCE

Berry Bros. & Rudd recently celebrated three centuries of trade; their shop at the lower end of St James's Street, built on the site of Henry VIII's royal tennis court, was first occupied in 1698.

Originally a grocery store which specialised in the sale of spices, tobacco, snuff, fine teas, and coffee, wine was most likely also available. By 1750 it was acknowledged as the best of London's grocers. Little seems to have changed within the

quaint front of shop with its uneven floors and dark wood panelling. The walls are lined, museum-like, with an array of old wine bottles and other memorabilia, while the cellars are approached through a trapdoor at one side of the shop.

John Lobb, the bespoke bootmaker, is just next door. The interior of the shop is redolent with the smell of expensive leather. A glass-fronted cabinet displays a rare assortment of footwear created by Lobb's since the shop began trading. Within the hushed, club-like premises, a group of skilled bootmakers are selecting and matching lengths of leather for the next pair of hand-crafted shoes, while others are putting the finishing touches to pairs of individual moulds which are numbered, ordered and stored in great racks in the basement of the shop.

James Lock & Co. can be found at No. 6 St James's Street and has been moulding and shaping hats for three centuries. It continues to be run in a personal and delightfully old-fashioned manner, with hats displayed on every surface and those

Cases of priceless wine (above and below) are laid down in the ancient cellars beneath the three hundred-year-old establishment of Berry Bros. & Rudd in St James's Street.

available "off the peg" stored in huge white cylindrical boxes the length of one wall. Orders are taken for anything from a top hat and a "Bowler" or "Coke" for the city gentleman, to a tweed cap and felt hat for the country-based client.

For those not able to afford the cost of custom-made clothing, shoes and accessories, there are alternatives a world away from the traditions of St James's and Bond Street, where designer suits and extraordinary bargains can be found. These are London's street markets and second-hand shops.

Racks of long Victorian shirts blow in the breeze along the Portobello Road in Notting Hill. Early Saturday mornings, the scavengers are out looking for bargains among the stalls selling bales of antique fabric and a plethora of textiles, while Camden Lock market is a riot of colour from the rack upon rack of cast-off clothing. And yet antique clothing is becoming increasingly difficult to find, the wonderful quality once available in the markets flagging under the pressure of too great a demand.

The answer for Stephen Calloway, writer and associate curator of the Victoria & Albert Museum, is to have his favourite articles of clothing, once discovered in these very markets, immaculately copied by a theatrical tailor he has discovered in Notting Hill. Steve Bell will turn his hand to anything, from simply copying a garment to drawing and designing a suit or coat from a mere description.

Stephen Calloway is a "dandy" in the true sense of the word, a man who studies

ostentatiously to dress elegantly and fashionably. Although in Stephen's case, "fashionable" should be read as individual. He is recognised everywhere he goes, his appearance an inspired and personal interpretation of the nineteenth century, complete with waxed moustache and beard trimmed to a point.

Other men, for whom a bygone era is not so attractive, commune at shops such as Voyage, which draws celebrities and rock musicians alike with its exotic Indian fabrics, unusual designs and signature velvet-trimmed cardigans. It is another of those "members only" elitist affairs at which the British seem to excel. Their new menswear and accessories shop, which recently started trading at the trendy end of the Fulham Road, has opened to a stream of new clients, eager to rifle through the Chinese waistcoats and shirts with cuffs trimmed in antique embroidery, velvets and silks of all colours imaginable.

Other original thinkers, such as Bertie Wooster in the Fulham Road, specialise in

Stephen Calloway is a writer and associate curator of the Victoria & Albert Museum. Seen here (left) in the first-floor drawing room of the large Georgian house he has recently acquired, and which he intends to restore one day.

Since the days of Beau Brummell, London has drawn gentlemen from around the world with its reputation for sartorial elegance. Upstairs on the first floor is the fitting room at bespoke tailor Timothy Everest's premises in Spitalfields (left). The waxed colour of old bones, it is dominated by a large three-sided mirror.

The eighteenth-century façade of James Lock & Co., hatters of St James (right) and the neat rows of large white circular boxes (facing page) in which all manner of gentlemen's hats are stored.

the resale of second-hand suits and dinner jackets. The occasional uniform and beautifully crafted old leather suitcase are also available. Country sales produce selections of hunting jackets and fishing coats and, like other sporting garments before them, create a transitory fashion item. These are available new, amongst others, from the various branches of Hacketts.

The English passion for the "hunting, shooting, fishing" way of life is reinforced by companies such as Purdey or Holland & Holland, makers and suppliers of the best guns in the country, who also cater for the sporting gentleman's taste in appropriate clothing and accessories for country pursuits. The sporting country look, epitomised and almost caricatured by the tweed jacket, has always been popular and, when used with individuality and a certain panache, can create a distinctive style.

The late Duke of Windsor had an interesting dress sense, with an eye for unusual combinations of fabrics and colours, as was revealed when, in early 1998, the contents of his ample wardrobe, together with the furniture and belongings from his house in the Bois de Boulogne, came up for sale at Sotheby's in New York. The Duke's erstwhile tailors, Hawes & Curtis of Jermyn Street, acquired a selection of his clothes at the auction and are now preparing to promote a "Duke of Windsor look".

LONDON RENDEZVOUS

A detail of Rex Whistler's mural (left), illustrating the adventures of the Duke and Duchess of Epicurania, which he painted in 1926–27 for the Tate Gallery Restaurant. Restricted by the opening hours of the museum, the restaurant serves lunch only but distinguishes itself with an excellent wine list.

The local street market is a hive of activity as Saturday morning's shoppers eagerly purchase their fruit and vegetables before the next rainstorm sends them running for cover. New faces and regulars are greeted by the stall-holders, a cheerful banter passing back and forth amongst the crowd as produce is weighed and paid for. Across London, this scene is repeated, the cosy familiarity of a local neighbourhood, belying the vast scale of the city and the apparent indifference Londoners have for each other.

Markets have always been the melting pots of society, where people of every nationality, creed and colour rub shoulders in the narrow streets, jostling for position amongst the stalls laden with provender, shouting and gesticulating for attention. The markets of Portobello Road in Notting Hill, Petticoat Lane in the East End, Chapel Street in Islington and others all over London, are natural meeting places, the crowds of shoppers swelled by those hunting for bargains from the barrows and small antique shops in adjoining streets.

Bargain-hunting is a natural weekend occupation in any city and London's reputation for antiques has the hardened expert out early to beat the rush. Alfie's Market in Church Street, Britain's largest covered antique market, is a close competitor to the Portobello Road market. Camden Passage in Islington has a vast selection of shops and stalls and, for the specially keen early-bird, Bermondsey Market at the crack of dawn on a Friday is the place to be.

If one finds nothing amongst the motley collection of stalls and barrows selling everything from silver and Victorian underwear to antique camera equipment, books and memorabilia, there are specialist shops and boutiques which tend to cluster around these markets, their cramped interior filled with objects and furniture, the darkest and least inviting corners normally giving up the most valuable treasures.

For those with less time, there are weekly auctions, such as Lots Road Auctions in Chelsea, where amateurs in search of furniture and carpets at the cheaper end of the scale, pit their nerves against the dealers and other experts hanging around the sale rooms.

The excitement can be intense and the build-up almost unbearable—items often heavily undervalued may go for high prices or, on the other hand, one might come away with an exceptional bargain. Certainly, at the grander auction houses of Sotheby's, Christie's, Phillips and Bonham's, experts and dealers often outnumber the casual punters, and it is fascinating to watch how the auctioneer controls the bidding and to catch the expressions on the faces of the crowd.

Spending money is a hunger-provoking occupation and the auction houses, all centrally located, are well served with good restaurants, pubs and bars in which to celebrate any acquisition or the profits from a sale. Sotheby's in Bond Street has recently opened its own cafe, where a light breakfast, lunch or tea is guaranteed to keep the customers happy between sales, while also providing an interesting new venue and meeting place for those shopping in Bond Street or nearby Oxford Street.

Two masterpieces of the Wallace Collection, *The Annunciation* by Philippe de Champaigne and an allegorical figure of River Tiber, attributed to Martin Carlier, are on display at Hertford House, the former private house of Sir Richard Wallace near Marble Arch (preceding double page).

Many museums and galleries are beginning to follow this trend for "in-house" restaurants and cafes. It is somehow reassuring to know that a morning spent in cerebral admiration of great works of art will be rewarded with something more than an uninspired sandwich.

In fact, it seems entirely natural to gravitate toward the cafes and tea rooms after any sort of cultural expedition, whether you are in need of restorative sustenance or not, and those bastions of British culture lacking this prerequisite rely heavily on the numerous small street cafes and restaurants which hover immediately beyond the gates of most of London's museums.

The restaurant at the Tate Gallery was probably the first to be located within a museum itself. Serving an English lunch, accompanied by a highly respected and innovative wine list, it is popular both with visitors to the Tate and local business executives alike. The low-ceilinged room is famous for the mural by Rex Whistler, painted in 1926–27, entitled *The Expedition in Pursuit of Rare Meats,* which illustrates the adventures of the Duke and Duchess of Epicurania. For those with less time than a serious lunch requires, the Tate also has a coffee shop next door to the restaurant where more simple fare can be enjoyed.

SECRET MUSEUMS

London is a city full of secret corners. The lives of the many individuals who have played an important part in its development, together with the style and imagination of a bygone age, are reflected in the numerous smaller and lesser known museums and galleries waiting to be discovered down some of the city's less frequented side streets. The most intriguing are those which were once private homes and where little seems to have changed since the owner closed the front door for the very last time.

Houses of famous men and women are distinguished by a blue plaque and the *Blue Plaque Guide,* published by the Greater London Council, provides an intriguing insight into the history of these properties. The houses of writers, playwrights, poets and artists have always inspired a certain voyeuristic curiosity. The majority are neither museums, nor open to the public, but English Heritage has developed an Open House Scheme which allows the public access to many of them over one long weekend each year, generally during the month of September.

The Georgian townhouse of Sir John Soane at Lincoln's Inn Fields in Holborn holds one of the most fascinating and eclectic private collections. Soane first came into the public eye when he was appointed architect to the Bank of England in 1788 and his reputation for collecting started gradually. In 1800, he built himself a country villa, Pitshanger Manor, in Ealing (see page 184) to house his objects. The London residence was extended into the building next door at No. 13, which was bought specifically to display the classical busts, statues, casts, paintings and treasures which Soane continued to accumulate at an alarming rate. Before he died in 1837,

The extraordinary Sculpture Gallery at the Sir John Soane's Museum in Lincoln's Inn Fields near Holborn is just one of the many exceptional rooms in the architect's Georgian home. Soane spent his life collecting classical busts, statues, casts, paintings and other treasures (right).

Soane obtained an Act of Parliament which preserved his houses and the collections as a public museum. Today, the singular yet striking facade of No. 13 still stands out from its neighbouring Georgian brick office buildings and subsequent modern additions. Inside, it has been left much as it might have been when Soane was still alive, an Aladdin's Cave of beautiful and curious objects.

The Victorian writer and historian, Thomas Carlyle, moved with his wife from

Scotland to Chelsea and took up residence in Cheyne Row in 1834. A modest terrace of Queen Anne townhouses just steps from the grandeur of Cheyne Walk, along Chelsea Embankment, No. 24 became the central pivot of literary and intellectual society for over forty years. Now managed by the National Trust, the mysterious creaking stairs and dark rooms filled with the Carlyles' Victorian furniture seem to have changed very little over the ensuing years. The attic study houses collections of books, letters and memorabilia, including Carlyle's volumes on Frederick the Great, which he spent twelve years in this eyrie compiling.

Sigmund Freud spent a very short time in London, after he fled Vienna in 1938 at the age of 82, and sought asylum along with many other Jewish *émigrés* in the area around Hampstead. He brought with him from Austria many of his belongings, including the carpets, furniture and antiques from his Viennese apartment. Freud died barely a year later and his daughter, Anna, continued to live in the house, leaving everything exactly as it was during her father's lifetime. His study, the couch draped in a heavy carpet after the Viennese fashion, is full of memorabilia. Phalanxes of tiny figures crowd his desk and the numerous glass-fronted cabinets, while one wall is lined from floor to ceiling with rows of

The attic study (left), where Thomas Carlyle worked for twelve years on his six-volume biography of Frederick the Great of Prussia, was created as an extension to the Chelsea house in 1853. The basement kitchen (below) has the original cast-iron saddle-back range with a self-supplying boiler and would have been the room in which the domestic servant slept.

F reud's desk and the unusual chair in his study and consulting room (above) look out over the quiet garden at the back of his house in Hampstead. He relinquished the apartment in Vienna where he had lived for decades and came to London with much of his furniture, carpets and relics.

Hampstead is also the location for another museum, that of the former home of the poet John Keats. Located in Well Walk, at the time a fashionable area for artists and writers, Keats was drawn to the area by its country air and the many like-minded and literary people he met there.

leather-bound books. Freud's home has been open to the public since 1985. Nothing has been added or removed since his death and it offers a touching insight into one of the greatest minds of the last century.

Another earlier resident of Hampstead, whose home has recently undergone extensive restoration and been re-opened to the public, was the nineteenth-century poet John Keats. He was part of the literary and artistic set of the time, whose members included the poet Percy Bysshe Shelley, the painters Benjamin Robert Haydon and Joseph Severn, and the critic and journalist Leigh Hunt.

Dr Samuel Johnson goes down in history as the man who compiled the first comprehensive English dictionary, which was published in 1755. His residence, in Gough Square, is located close to Fleet Street, home until recently of the British newspaper industry, and was singled out by Dr Johnson for its proximity to the printers he had chosen to work with on the dictionary. It is one of only a handful of residen-

tial houses of its period to have survived in the City.

"Square" is perhaps too grand a description for the small cobbled courtyard on which the house stands; rather it is typical of the labyrinth of narrow alleyways and yards which criss-cross the area. The panelled rooms in the four-storey property, painted in soft shades of grey and pastel, are remarkably under-furnished. Apparently, Johnson's great height and girth took their toll on his furniture and there was barely a chair with four good legs left by the time he had finished with them.

Artists have long been associated with an enviably romantic lifestyle and Leighton House in Kensington is one of the few purpose-built artists' studios, albeit on a very grand scale, which is open to the public.

T he front parlour at Samuel Johnson's house in Gough Square (below) is used today to display the third edition of *A Dictionary of the English Language*, published in 1755, which he compiled in the garret at the top of the house. Above the fireplace hangs the portrait of Francis Barber, a Jamaican boy who became Dr. Johnson's servant and subsequently his principal heir.

The Arab Hall at Leighton House, near Holland Park in Kensington is intended to evoke the world of the Arabian Nights and the magic of the Orient, with alcoves of Cairene latticework and walls covered with floral patterned tiles from Cairo, Damascus and Rhodes (left).

Old Battersea House, open to the public by appointment, is a private home owned by Christopher Forbes, the son of the American publisher who rescued the property from ruin over twenty years ago. In one corner of the drawing room (top right) hangs the famous painting by John Everett Millais *Trust Me,* together with other paintings by Rebecca Solomon, Byam Shaw, Augustus Leopold and Arthur Hughes.

Described as "the unique expression of the taste and sensibility of one man," it was designed for the artist Lord Leighton by his friend George Aitchison and was originally intended as a working studio as well as a private home devoted to art. It is best known for the exotic Arab Hall, added to the house in 1877, which has become its centrepiece. Created as a setting for the Isnik tiles which Leighton had acquired on his travels, Aitchison based his design on the banqueting room at La Zisa, a Moorish palace in Palermo. Nothing prepares the visitor for its unexpected and breathtaking beauty, the density of its colour and the quality of the tiles.

On the south bank of the Thames in Battersea, Old Battersea House is one of the few late seventeenth-century survivors in a sea of modern buildings and is purported to have been designed by Christopher Wren as the dower house to the old manor house of Battersea. Restored in the 1970s by the American publisher, Malcolm Forbes, Old Battersea House is still owned and used by his family. It houses an exceptional collection of Pre-Raphaelite paintings and lustreware belonging to the De Morgan Foundation as well as the Forbes Magazine Collection of early Victorian paintings, which includes works by Edwin Landseer, William Holman Hunt and John Everett Millais.

On a grander scale, another private collection is housed at Hertford House in Manchester Square, an oasis of peace next to the bustle of Oxford Street. Bequeathed to the nation in 1897, the Wallace Collection reflects the unique, Anglo-

French nineteenth-century taste of the fourth Marquess of Hertford. One of the greatest private collections of French eighteenth-century paintings, porcelain and furniture outside Paris, nothing is ever loaned nor pieces from other museums

Hertford House was built as Manchester House in 1776 for the fourth Duke of Manchester. Designed by Joshua Brown, it was leased by the second Marquess of Hertford in 1797 and between 1836 and 1850 the house served as the French Embassy. After 1850 the property was used primarily to store the vast collection of works of art of the fourth Marquess and today its rather austere façade (centre left) conceals a sumptuous interior, the backdrop for The Wallace Collection. The grandeur of the Front State Room (below) is overwhelming.

ever borrowed, ensuring the collection remains original and unspoilt. Raised in Paris by his grandmother, the illegitimate son of the fourth Marquess of Hertford, Sir Richard Wallace inherited his father's collection, a French chateau and a Paris apartment in 1870. In 1872 he took up residence in Manchester Square bringing with him

from Paris many of the finest works of art, which are now displayed in magnificent surroundings.

Far removed from the grandeur of these latter properties, both in distance and origin, the Geffrye Museum is situated in Hackney, east of Islington, the centre of the furniture and cabinet makers of London. It was originally the site of fourteen alms houses which were built in 1715 under the bequest of Sir Robert Geffrye, a former Lord Mayor of London, to encourage aging and ailing workers away from the city to a peaceful retirement in the country.

That countryside was to be gradually absorbed back into the slums of London and in 1914 the buildings were converted into a museum with permanent displays of fully furnished rooms dating from Elizabethan times to the 1930s. It is the only museum of its kind in England which is dedicated to the developing styles and idiosyncrasies in interior design over the centuries. The detail and historical accuracy is fascinating; students and visitors alike can study the colour schemes used in the blue Regency drawing room and the remarkable furniture which fills the Victorian parlour. A recent grant has resulted in the construction of a new circular building in the grounds, which will bring the exhibits right up to the twenty-first century.

The Regency Room (far left and right) at the Geffrye Museum in Hackney located to the north of the City, represents the drawing room of a London town house 1800–1830. The arrangement of the furniture reflects a change towards a less formal domestic way of life, with upholstered, comfortable sofas and the use of exotic wood and stains, all characteristic of the Regency style.
The wallpaper with its stencilled pattern is a replica based on a fragment found in Lauderdale House in Highgate, *c.* 1820.

The Stuart Room (below) represents a parlour from about 1660 to 1680, furnished as the private room of a wealthy, educated gentleman for study and informal entertaining. The oak panelling and carved detail, together with the replica ceiling plaster, is taken from the Master's Parlour in the Pewterers Hall, *c.* 1668.

later additions by Sir Christopher Wren. The country palace for successive generations of English monarchs, the establishment of Hampton Court encouraged other courtiers and aristocrats to seek estates nearby. In addition to enjoying the gardens and sumptuous interiors, the public can also take advantage of the annual flower show and the open-air concerts which are held during the summer months in the quadrangle. In imitation of the tradition established at Glyndebourne near Lewes in Sussex, where a festival of opera and classical music is held every summer, spectators arrive equipped with hampers and refreshments, to enjoy a picnic on the lawns as dusk descends before the start of the evening performance.

Osterley Park, has seen many changes over the years, the most famous being the intervention of Robert Adam in 1761. His innovative decorating schemes transformed the house into one of the great showplaces of his work, and today visitors can still marvel at the magnificent rooms with neo-classical ceilings and furniture.

Robert Adam designed the Etruscan Dressing Room at Osterley Park in 1772 (right). Located on the outskirts of West London, the residence has survived remarkably in its original form. One of several properties which were built or aggrandised for courtiers and aristocrats following the royal patronage of Hampton Court, Osterley Park is located close to Syon House, Robert Adam's masterpiece.

The ceiling of The Great Hall at Ham House, a Jacobean manor house near the Thames at Richmond (above), was pierced around the beginning of the eighteenth century to create the present hall and first-floor gallery. Under the National Trust, Ham House is one of the few properties of the period to have survived with its original furniture and textiles intact, offering a true reflection of seventeenth-century life.

LONDON'S COUNTRY ESTATES

Lovers of English history should head west to the outskirts of the city, where the country estates and gardens of Hampton Court (1514), Syon House (1594), Ham House (1610), Osterley Park (1577) and Chiswick House (1725) afford a visual insight into the architectural history of both royal and aristocratic houses. The erstwhile country residences and follies of many of England's grand families, today the houses and grounds of these estates are open to the public, their parks and gardens wonderful places to walk in an atmosphere laden with cultural heritage.

Hampton Court is located on the banks of the Thames and boasts some of the finest Tudor architecture in England, as well as

Pitshanger Manor in Ealing in West London was the country villa which Sir John Soane built for himself at the turn of the 19th century. The Library (left) and a detail of the Breakfast Room ceiling (above) are illustrated here.

The Hall at Osterley Park (left) was designed by Robert Adam in 1767 to replace the earlier hall which was demolished when the portico was created. It was used as a reception room and occasional dining room and is decorated with stucco panels of military trophies.

A row of statues, half hidden in a thick hedge leads up to the Palladian wing of Chiswick House in West London (far left and below right). Designed as a rich man's folly, the white stucco façade of the main rotunda is ornately decorated with graceful columns (left), and the interior, although sparsely furnished, has been beautifully restored and gilded. The simple design of the annex to the rotunda is by contrast unadorned (bottom left), while the park is still full of surprises.

Given a complete makeover by Robert Adam, prior to Osterley Park, Syon House is still the seat of the Duke of Northumberland. Adam worked for several years, creating within the existing structure new suites of rooms, the most famous of which is the Great Hall. Standing in an elegant setting on the banks of the Thames, Syon House's botanical gardens were opened to the public in 1837 and the first national centre of gardening was set up in the mid-1960s. Its conservatory, designed by Charles Fowler and constructed of gun metal and Bath stone, is thought to have inspired Joseph Paxton in the design of Crystal Palace, built for the Great Exhibition of 1851.

Chiswick House was modelled on Palladio's Villa Rotonda at Vicenza and built in 1725 under the instruction of the third Earl of Burlington, who employed William Kent to create the spectacular plaster ceilings and fireplace. Burlington used Chiswick as a pleasure palace for entertaining friends and displaying works of art. He filled the gardens with follies, many of which have not survived, but enough ruins, columns and obelisks remain to fire the imagination.

Sir Terence Conran wheels his trolley around the racks of meticulously placed wine bottles at The Bluebird Gourmet Shop, an extensive gourmet complex on the fashionable King's Road (left). A former ambulance station, it now features a cobbled courtyard, with a central display of fresh fruit and vegetables and a colourful flower stand. Tables and chairs of the coffee shop fill rapidly and through the open windows of the restaurant on the first floor, the clinking of glasses and murmur of voices drift down to street level.

Bargains await the early birds at Bermondsey Market on the South Bank (right), where the antique stalls which appear every Friday morning constitute one of London's most important street markets (photograph by Henry Wilson).

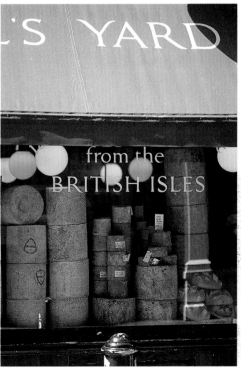

Tom's Delicatessen (bottom left), owned by Tom Conran, is the trendiest spot for cappuccino in the centre of Notting Hill. A narrow shop filled with fresh produce, patisseries and unusual specialities, it is always full of locals and on a Saturday morning the small coffee shop at the rear is a favourite for fans of the Portobello Road antique market.

Neal's Yard in Covent Garden (bottom right) is the location for a number of small specialist boutiques set slightly apart from the general bustle and chaos of the central square. Among them is this shop which specialises in cheese from all over the British Isles and, even better, offers the chance to sample them.

CAFES AND TEA HOUSES

The trend for street cafes is only just starting to catch on. The unreliability of the weather is often blamed, but it may have more to do with British temperament than anything else. A direct result of the increasing number of Europeans taking up residence in London, the city is at last letting its hair down. More cafes are in evidence and, during the summer months at least, they spill out onto the pavements.

Yet the narrow, traffic-laden streets of London do not lend themselves so easily to

Tea at Claridge's (right), the celebrated hotel in Brook Street, is served by a frock-coated waiter in an elegant ante-room with faux marble columns and tapestry armchairs. The tradition of afternoon tea is generally upheld by many of the exclusive hotels in London, such as Brown's in Albermarle Street off Piccadilly, as well as by various tea shops and coffee houses, the most well-known of these being Fortnum & Mason.

this Parisian way of doing things. Licensing restrictions often make it impossible to have more than a couple of tables outside, and many cafes are serving *al fresco* customers in converted back gardens and courtyards, where the fumes and proximity of passers-by are less likely to spoil the moment.

Many of the new wave of trendy cafes are French, combining chic, modern premises with the sale of cakes and patis-

series, strong coffee and other Gallic delights. Franchises are popping up on convenient street corners, as fewer Londoners seem to partake of breakfast at home, preferring the convenience of a coffee and croissant "to go".

Other cafes, such as Tom's in Notting Hill, double as delicatessens, offering endless temptations to take home or enjoy at one of the intimate tables. Small restaurants have also got in on the act, supplementing their income by serving coffee throughout the day.

The English have a reputation when it comes to afternoon tea, a custom which is alleged to have started in the early 1800s, with Anna, seventh Duchess of Bedford. To ward off hunger pangs until it was time for dinner, she would have tea and cakes served at around five o'clock in the afternoon.

Today, the tradition of "proper" afternoon tea is perpetuated by many of London's finest hotels, such as Brown's or Claridge's, where tea is served amidst the imposing grandeur of columned foyers and gracious ante-rooms. The smaller townhouse hotels, such as Eleven Cadogan Gardens, serve tea in the cosy intimacy of the drawing room. Such a traditional English tea would include wafer-thin cucumber sandwiches and scones, hot from the oven, served with butter and strawberry jam or dollops of cream.

The most famous of all the tea houses in London must be Fortnum & Mason, the store on Piccadilly which was opened in 1770 by Charles Fortnum, once a footman in the household of George III.

Eleven Cadogan Gardens is a discreet hotel in an elegant terrace of Victorian red-brick houses situated around a garden square in Chelsea. Tea can be enjoyed in the comfortable drawing room, where an open fire burns during the winter.

Hotel residents are invited to help themselves to a slice of the "cake of the day", or they may decide to order cucumber sandwiches and scones and cream.

LONDON'S PUBS AND BARS

At one time the temperature of the city was regularly taken at London's public houses, or pubs. A veritable bastion of the male right to freedom of expression, opinions would be voiced, politics and sport discussed. The original definition as "a house in respect of which a licence has been obtained for the consumption of intoxicating liquors," now seems very outdated.

Today, the pub scene and London's drinking habits, in particular, have undergone an enormous shake up.

Just as London's villages reflect the style and preferences of their inhabitants, so pubs and bars are barometers of change in an area, providing instant clues as to the cultural mix and interests of their clientele.

London's pubs are various and plentiful. French-style bars, like the Dome (left) with branches all over central London, contrast starkly with the dark, brooding interiors of The Black Friar near the Thames at Blackfriars Bridge in the City (far left) decorated with bronze friezes of monks.

The variety of London's pubs can be loosely categorised. There is the "local"—impervious to change, design trends or style gurus—which continues to serve pints of warm beer to an undemanding crowd of regulars. There are the "themed" pubs, owned by large breweries which specialise in that "olde worlde" look and fill their buildings with unnecessary accessories and knick-knacks to lend an atmosphere of phoney nostalgia. Food with no frills—traditional "pub grub"—is the order of the

The Paradise Bar (left and below) at the top end of Notting Hill is a large converted pub, with rough wood floors and great atmosphere. The front room is taken up by a large bar with a lively restaurant at the back and additional rooms for live music on the first floor. Sunday lunch is a speciality and can go on all afternoon.

day, a background noise of endless taped muzak an unmistakable identification.

There are independent pubs, so-called free houses, which specialise in a wide variety of real ale and good beer. There are pubs that exhibit local artwork, theatre pubs, those which hold comedy nights, poetry readings and literary evenings, or present jazz and live music. In fact, the pub is the mainstay of most Londoners' idea of entertainment and a good night out.

A more recent innovation is the pub with a pared down, modern interior, which has been transforming empty premises all over London, attracting the cool, young set—the drinkers of tomorrow. Warm beer is losing out to designer-label lager from the continent, while high volume, storming dance music is replacing the local live band that churns out seventies-style rock.

Wine bars are also picking up on this modern trend, the former candle-lit basement City "dives" being replaced by those with sleek chrome and pale wood interiors. Imaginative wine lists reflect newly-acquired knowledge and confidence while patrons take interest in what is actually being served.

Bars, unlike pubs, are more susceptible to the waves of popularity and style mania which wash over London at regular intervals. Up-to-the-minute interiors, the latest

in trendy seating, cool lighting and expensive decor attract the "in crowd" within hours of a new bar opening its doors. A demanding clientele will make or break a bar within a week, the hottest venues vacillating between the chic designer haunts of new hotels and the more recent style-setters of the restaurant-bars.

Restaurants

Rules (left) in Covent Garden is London's oldest restaurant. Its Victorian interior, filled with paintings, cartoons and memorabilia, has played host over the years to writers, actors and artists of all descriptions.

Albert Roux said recently that a city's success can be measured in the number of new restaurants which open each week; they act as a barometer, determining the mood. In London the mood must be optimistic, since the city has witnessed an unprecedented explosion of restaurants over the last few years.

Londoners are eating out more than ever before and the choice is limitless. Chefs and restaurateurs have become minor celebrities, new premises heralded with so much media attention that capacity seatings and instant exclusivity are more or less guaranteed.

London has always been renowned for the variety of restaurants available and the choice of ethnic alternatives ensures every palate and eccentricity of diet is catered for. As the clientele has become more demanding and knowledgeable, so the English reputation for poor quality restaurants is being shed, London's culinary talents currently ranking alongside those of Paris.

A great deal has been done over the last twenty years to improve the options for dining out for Londoners. Spearheaded by

Simpson's-in-the-Strand (top) is one of those traditional, panelled, club-style restaurants a few doors down from The Savoy where one can discover the pleasures of a proper full English breakfast. Lunch and dinner are also served, with roast meats offered by the chef from a silver trolley.

The Cow, a traditional pub in Notting Hill (centre), serves a simple choice of lunch and dinner at the back end of the room, while those who simply want a drink pack the bar. Its speciality is a lunch of oysters washed down with a pint of Guinness.

Blakes is the creation of designer Anouska Hempel, who has applied her innate sense of style to this smart hotel, popular with rock and film stars, in a residential street of terraced houses in South Kensington. Each of the bedrooms is furnished differently, and the sophisticated restaurant (bottom) combines delicious food with stylish ambience.

individuals such as Sir Terence Conran, who has introduced a new style of eatery to a young and demanding market, the restaurants currently finding favour have several elements in common: the food is new, interesting and delicious and the setting is chic, cool and fashionable. The chance of rubbing shoulders with the rich and famous is also part of the attraction and can mean a six-month wait for a suitable table. London is on show and exhibitionism begins in its restaurants.

Like the city's pubs and bars, restaurants fall into several categories. The bastions of tradition, with a loyal clientele, preserve the best of British cooking, impeccable service and fine table linen. Many of these are inevitably linked to London's top hotels.

The club, that very English preserve of secrecy and exclusivity, has extended into the realm of the restaurant. Eating clubs are becoming increasingly popular, where

"recognisable faces", harassed and constantly chased by the media, can eat in guaranteed privacy and businessmen can close a deal over a quiet lunch in an exclusive atmosphere.

Restaurant clubs, however, differ from gentlemen's clubs in several important ways. Membership is not limited to men only, food is an important commodity and many of the members have joined with its ultimate appreciation in mind. In response to this new wave of connoisseur, other well-known clubs are sprucing up their act, members are becoming more discerning and menus consequently more ambitious.

From the simplest and cheapest bowl of noodles in unpretentious surroundings, to the latest craze for plates delivered by conveyor-belt in high-tech chic, London's restaurants differ from their European counterparts in one significant fashion. The ambience is as important as the food. Thus, the decision where to eat out is complicated not only by the ethnic diversity, but also by one's mood at the time.

Beach Blanket Babylon in Ledbury Road at the centre of Notting Hill (left and centre) is famous for its eccentric interior decoration, while The Vendome in Dover Street off Piccadilly (right) has a chic West End look with its glossy red walls and trendy banquettes.

The modern surroundings of the Reading Room at The Cobden Club in Notting Hill (below) provide members with a place for quiet contemplation. Occupying the first and second floors of the Cobden Working Men's Club, designers Matthew Godley and Justin Meath Baker have created an environment within the original building. It features a magnificent Victorian theatre on the second floor with a 30-foot bar and floor to ceiling mirrors around the walls.

HOTELS

A secret ambition of many Londoners after a night on the town is to simply not go home, but check into one of the city's luxury hotels—to be served breakfast in bed or champagne in a marble bathroom and to sleep between linen sheets. Whether it follows a night at the theatre, the opera, a rock concert or a simple dinner, the choice of hotels is infinite and there is one to suit every taste.

Staff trained at The Savoy have influenced the standard of hotels around the world and London continues to enjoy a reputation for excellence in both service and tradition which is perpetuated by the many small, privately owned hotels as well as by the larger chains.

Like the city's restaurants, there are hotels to appeal to everyone's aspirations. The true English classics, their names rolling off the tongues of any visitor to London; the small, discreet establishments where guests are neither acknowledged nor publicised; the places conversely where people wish to be seen; or the best Bed & Breakfasts in town.

Hotels and their reputations come and go, occasionally an exceptional newcomer joining the established list. Many are now associated with leading restaurants, while others have trendy bars, and all are attracting a new and more permanent clientele almost as often as the transitory tourist and businessman.

London provokes a reaction in resident and visitor alike. It awakens our senses, encourages our affection and nurtures our ambition. Visitors are often challenged by its hidden treasures, sometimes overwhelmed by its grandeur, uncertain of its soul, yet come away with a shared sense of discovery, an intimacy with a city and its residents, whose secrets only many return trips will ultimately reveal.

The traditional formality of The Connaught (above), located near Grosvenor and Berkeley Squares, continues to be the preferred address in London of the city's more demanding visitors. Renowned for its standard of impeccable service and for The Grill Restaurant, this hotel represents the epitome of English quality.

Just the name "Ritz" conjures up the glamorous days of London society. The hotel on Piccadilly has been forever synonymous with wealth and style. The Restaurant (right) is the ultimate in grandeur, its decoration richer and more opulent than any of the other reception rooms, with a panelled wall-lining of different marbles, elaborate light fittings and elegant chandeliers.

The Portobello in Notting Hill (centre and bottom left) is a favourite hideaway for many in the public eye. Its rooms are flamboyantly decorated, some with four-poster beds, others extravagantly draped in lengths of fabric, but all fitted with Victorian free-standing baths and old-fashioned copper plumbing.

The beautiful "Butter Yellow Library" (following page), formerly owned by Nancy Lancaster, is now the main showroom for the range of French and English antiques sold through Sybil Colefax & John Fowler in Brook Street.

VISITOR'S GUIDE

London continues to surprise and enchant both visitor and resident alike. Its spirit reflects a city that is constantly evolving. And yet, London can represent all that is traditional in its ostensibly rigid adherence to custom and ceremony. Modern Londoners seek to strike a balance between old and new, and this happy coupling manifests itself in a city of seeming contradictions. To get to know London, one has to consider and to appreciate both aspects of life in the city.

London can daunt not only the casual visitor but also the established resident. Its vastness can be overwhelming. Well-served by public transport, it can, none the less, take over an hour to cross the extreme limits of the city.

This Visitor's Guide, therefore, serves to break up London into manageable chunks. Villages and neighbourhoods are grouped together here by geographic position and by the social status they often share.

The following list of hotels, restaurants, pubs, bars, cafés, antique shops and garden centres is far from exhaustive. Rather, it aims to reveal some of the more interesting places currently finding favour—whether they be long-standing institutions or the latest in trendy settings.

Likewise, an effort has been made to select a few of the more unusual museums and galleries to be found in the capital. Whatever one's pleasure, London offers such a multitude of experiences— cultural, culinary and cosmopolitan—that leave visitor and resident yearning to discover more.

Kensington, Holland Park, Notting Hill and Bayswater

HOTELS

ABBEY COURT HOTEL
20 Pembridge Gardens, W2
Tel: 0171 221 7518
This Victorian townhouse is located on a quiet residential street close to the Portobello Road and a plethora of Notting Hill restaurants. It has a choice of twenty-two rooms, all tastefully furnished, each with a marble bathroom. Breakfast, light meals and tea are served in the conservatory.

THE HALCYON HOTEL
81 Holland Park, W11
Tel: 0171 727 7288
The pink façade of this Victorian double-fronted house sets it apart from its residential neighbours. With a variety of luxuriously decorated bedrooms, it also has a popular restaurant which is open to non-residents.

THE HEMPEL
Hempel Garden Square
31–35 Craven Hill Gardens, W2
Tel: 0171 298 9000
Situated just north of Hyde Park in a typical London square of white stucco-fronted houses, nothing prepares the guest for the unexpected minimalist design behind this traditional exterior. The inspiration of Anouska Hempel, the hotel is designed around clearly defined spaces, oriental in atmosphere and influence. Each of the three floors of suites and bedrooms offers a monochrome choice of design.

THE PORTOBELLO HOTEL
22 Stanley Gardens, W11
Tel: 0171 727 2777
Ideally located and a stone's throw from the Portobello Road antiques market, the hotel's twenty-two rooms are individually decorated, many with four-poster beds and Victorian baths. A favourite with celebrities from the world of music and fashion.

RESTAURANTS

ASSAGGI
39 Chepstow Place, W2
Tel: 0171 792 5501
This small restaurant, located above a pub, consists of a collection of bare wooden tables and chairs in a bright setting, reminiscent of a school classroom. Its limited menu is explained to the guests personally by the chef, who also gives his recommendations for wine. Assaggi's offers some of the best Italian food currently to be found in London.

BOOKS FOR COOKS
4 Blenheim Crescent, W11
Tel: 0171 221 1992
A treat any day of the week, but particularly on Saturdays, this small bookshop has space for a tiny restaurant amidst the tight rows of cookery books.

BRASSERIE DU MARCHE AUX PUCES
349 Portobello Road, W10
Tel: 0181 968 5828
Very French, this bistro located on a corner at the top end of the Portobello Road has few tables and is nearly always packed. Food is authentic and delicious.

COSTA'S FISH RESTAURANT
18 Hillgate Street, W8
Tel: 0171 727 4310
Well-known and popular in Notting Hill, Costa's serves classic English fish and chips.

I-THAI
The Hempel
31–35 Craven Hill Gardens, W2
Tel: 0171 298 9000
A fusion of Thai, Italian and Japanese cooking in a minimalist setting of opaque glass panels, ebony tables and white walls. The same eye for detail which epitomises the hotel has been given to the presentation and quality of every dish and the interesting menu is accompanied by a carefully selected wine list.

JIMMY BEEZ

303 Portobello Road, W10
Tel: 0181 964 9100
A great place to hang out at weekends, this diner is very popular with locals for brunch.

JULIE'S RESTAURANT

135 Portland Road, W11
Tel: 0171 229 8331
Julie's has been a London favourite since the 1970s, its seductive decorative style reaffirming it as a perfect setting for a romantic dinner.

KENSINGTON PLACE

201–205 Kensington Church Street, W8
Tel: 0171 727 318
With a modern location at Notting Hill Gate, this bustling, noisy and extremely popular brasserie serves a selection of good British food.

LAUNCESTON PLACE

1a Launceston Place, W8
Tel: 0171 937 6912
Affiliated with Kensington Place, this restaurant has a more traditional drawing room atmosphere, combined with delicious British cooking and good service.

MAGGIE JONES'S

6 Old Court Place, W8
Tel: 0171 937 6462
Good home cooking and a packed, cosy atmosphere make this restaurant particularly popular in winter. The menu offers a wide variety of good British fare and some traditional puddings.

MALABAR

27 Uxbridge Street, W8
Tel: 0171 727 8800
An Indian restaurant with a Mediterranean atmosphere just off Notting Hill Gate, which serves good, colourful curries.

MAS CAFE

6–8 All Saints Road, W11
Tel: 0171 243 0969
Famous for its weekend brunch, which attracts crowds to its friendly relaxed Notting Hill setting.

OSTERIA BASILICO

29 Kensington Park Road, W11
Tel: 0171 727 9957
Fresh Italian food and home-made pizzas pack the locals into this fun restaurant at the Portobello Road end of this busy street.

PHARMACY

Restaurant and Bar
150 Notting Hill Gate, W11
Tel: 0171 221 2442
A Damien Hirst design featuring an interesting bar—with clinically intoxicating drinks—and a restaurant upstairs serving modern British food.

ROYAL CHINA

13 Queensway, W2
Tel: 0171 221 2535
The decoration may be over the top but this Chinese restaurant in Bayswater serves the best dim sum in London–only available at lunchtime. It is as popular with the Chinese as it is with the locals, which is always a good sign.

STICKY FINGERS

1a Phillimore Gardens, W8
Tel: 0171 938 5338
This Kensington diner was opened some time ago by ex-Rolling Stone, Bill Wyman. A favourite with children of all ages, the burgers are a speciality.

THE SUGAR CLUB

33 All Saints Road, W11
Tel: 0171 221 3844
This trendy restaurant in the heart of Notting Hill concentrates on imaginative dishes from the Pacific Rim.

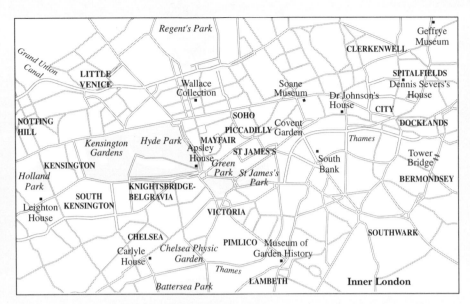

The atmosphere is modern and helped by a courtyard in summer.

WIZ

123a Clarendon Road, W11
Tel.: 0171 229 1500
A new tapas bar/restaurant which offers over 75 dishes from around the world in a Moroccan atmosphere, with large colourful cushions scattered around the walls, and relaxed and friendly service.

BARS

192

192 Kensington Park Road, W11
Tel: 0171 229 0482
Modern British cooking, a good wine list and a convivial atmosphere continue to lure the Notting Hill set to this wine bar, which also has a good restaurant.

BEACH BLANKET BABYLON

45 Ledbury Road, W11
Tel: 0171 229 2907
A funky and fun interior with a quirky restaurant at the rear attracts a trendy young crowd of the Notting Hill scene.

JULIE'S WINE BAR

137 Portland Road, W11
Tel: 0171 727 7985
Located next door to Julie's Restaurant this well-established bar offers a selection of reasonably-priced food and a great afternoon tea in a seventies atmosphere

PARADISE BAR

19 Kilburn Lane, W10
Tel: 0181 969 0098
Although technically not in Notting Hill, this bar and restaurant at the top of Ladbroke Grove offer a relaxed combination of music, food and drink and Sunday lunch can go on all day.

PORTOBELLO GOLD

95 Portobello Road, W11
Tel: 0171 460 4900
A Bohemian atmosphere and delicious oysters maintain the popularity of this bar at the Notting Hill end of the Portobello Road.

WINE FACTORY

294 Westbourne Grove, W11
Tel: 0171 229 1877
The Wine Factory sells decent bottles of wine at shop prices with a wide range of producers on

offer. Pizza or a simple dish of pasta is an easy accompaniment. The modern surroundings are stark with huge plate glass windows.

PUBS

BABUSHKA

41 Tavistock Crescent, W11
Tel: 0171 727 9250
A chrome bar made up of arched mirrors with fifty-six back-lit bottles of vodka, red walls and funky music distinguish this pub in Notting Hill. Poets and DJs perform on different nights and there is even ballroom dancing on Saturday afternoons.

THE COW

89 Westbourne Park Road, W11
Tel: 0171 221 0021
This trendy Notting Hill location offers a selection of delicious seafood to accompany a pint of Guinness or beer in a traditional pub setting. Upstairs, there is a separate restaurant, ideal for larger groups in search of simple fare.

THE LADBROKE ARMS
54 Ladbroke Road, W11
Tel: 0171 727 6648
A traditional pub, small but well arranged, serving a variety of draught beers and good wines. A selection of good European food is particularly popular on a Sunday at lunch and the speciality of the house is the wonderful sausages.

THE PRINCE BONAPARTE
80 Chepstow Road, W2
Tel: 0171 229 5912
A lively and trendy pub in Bayswater, it has a reputation for excellent and unusual pub food which includes fresh salads and soups.

THE SCARSDALE
23a Edwardes Square, W8
Tel: 0171 937 1811
The location of this pub is everything, with a tiny garden overlooking the best of Kensington's residential squares.

THE WESTBOURNE
101 Westbourne Park Villas, W2
Tel: 0171 221 1332
This hip pub continues to pack in the drinkers who crowd the pavement in front of the premises. In addition to the usual line of beers and wines, it also offers unusually tasty and reasonably cheap food.

THE WINDSOR CASTLE
114 Campden Hill Road, W8
Tel: 0171 727 8491
This pub boasts one of the best beer gardens in London. Walled and paved, with a huge and ancient tree in its centre, customers can enjoy a selection of good London beer, along with European brands, and food which is value for money.

DELICATESSENS, COFFEE AND JUICE BARS

ARGILE GALLERY
7 Blenheim Crescent, W11
Tel: 0171 792 0888
In the same short street as Books for Cooks and the Travel Bookshop, this coffee shop/gallery is an essential stop on a trip down the Portobello Road.

THE COURTYARD CAFE
59a Portobello Road, W11
Tel: 0171 221 8416
Hidden in a small and pretty courtyard, this cafe is an unexpected respite from the rigours of shopping in Notting Hill and is good value for money.

FAT RASCALS
52 Ledbury Road, W11
Tel: 0171 792 8843
Located in this very trendy street of boutiques, antique shops and designer florists, this coffee house takes its name from the scone-like buns which originated in Yorkshire. Its coffee is freshly roasted around the corner by the Coffee Store on the Portobello Road. A selection of sandwiches and cakes is available.

FELICITOUS
19 Kensington Park Road, W11
Tel: 0171 243 4050
On a street in Notting Hill, which is already the location for a number of popular restaurants, this delicatessen is the brainchild of Felicity Osborne, whose name is more readily connected with the world of interior design than with food.

LISBOA PATISSERIE
57 Golborne Road, W10
Tel: 0181 968 5242
At the top end of Portobello Road, on a street famous for its Portuguese coffee houses, this is by far the best. Full of local characters from the moment it opens, it serves delicious coffee and the best custard tarts in London.

MANZARA
24 Pembridge Street, W11
Tel: 0171 727 3062
This simple bistro, also off Notting Hill Gate, offers some of the cheapest and best Turkish food in London, but is best known for its pastries baked on the premises. The coffee menu is extensive.

MR. CHRISTIAN'S
11 Elgin Crescent, W11
Tel: 0171 229 0501
A local favourite among the Notting Hill *cognoscenti*, Mr. Christian's offers a mouth-watering selection of exotic bread, cheese, salami and other tasty goodies.

PLANET ORGANIC
42 Westbourne Grove, W2
Tel: 0171 221 7171
Ostensibly an organic food store, Planet Organic has a stand-up juice bar offering endless combinations of organic fruit and vegetables, together with organic tea and a delicious range of coffees made with soya milk.

TOM'S
226 Westbourne Grove, W11
Tel: 0171 221 8818
An upmarket delicatessen owned by Tom Conran which offers a wide selection of homemade dishes, specialist pastas, bread, etc. There is also seating in the shop for customers to linger over a large frothy cappuccino or a light snack. In the summer, capacity is increased by the small garden at the rear of the premises.

ANTIQUE SHOPS, DEALERS AND MARKETS

BAZAR
82 Golbourne Road, W10
Tel: 0181 969 6262
Decorative French country furniture, kitchen antiques, and so on.

THE CROSS
141 Portland Road, W11
Tel: 0171 727 676
Appliqué blankets, antique ticking, cushions and glass, recycled wooden picture frames and other decorative accessories.

DANIEL MANKOWITZ
208a Westbourne Grove, W11
Tel: 0171 229 9270
Unusual early and decorative furniture, textiles and paintings.

GRAHAM & GREENE
4 & 7 Elgin Crescent, W11
Tel: 0171 727 4594
Two shops in the heart of Notting Hill are crammed with kitchenware, gear for the garden, lighting, furniture and accessories.

HASLAM & WHITEWAY
105 Kensington Church Street, W8
Tel: 0171 229 1145
British furniture and decorative arts dating from 1850 to 1930.

MANUEL CASTILHO
53 Ledbury Road, W11
Tel: 0171 221 4928
Early continental furniture, mainly Portuguese and Spanish, painted furniture and mirrors.

ORMONDE GALLERY
156 Portobello Road, W11
Tel: 0171 229 9800
Assortment of oriental antiques, lacqueur cupboards and objets from mainland China.

PETER FARLOW
189 Westbourne Grove, W11
Tel: 0171 229 8306
Nineteenth-century Gothic revival and Arts & Crafts. The Coach House behind the shop has three other dealers offering the best of the nineteenth century.

PORTOBELLO ROAD MARKET
Portobello Road and Westbourne Grove, W11
World famous antiques market (Saturdays only) with hundreds of stalls, shops and little arcades. The neighbouring boutiques and antique shops along Westbourne Grove, Ledbury Road and Golbourne Road are also open during the week.

THEMES & VARIATIONS
231 Westbourne Grove, W11
Tel: 0171 727 5531
Post-war and pop art design. Exclusive agents for Fornasetti. Contemporary artists include André Dubreuil, Danny Lane and Tom Dixon.

UNIVERSAL PROVIDERS
86 Golbourne Road, W10
Tel: 0181 960 3736
French metal cafe chairs and other furniture, old shop fittings.

GARDENING SHOPS AND CENTRES

AVANT GARDEN
77 Ledbury Road, W11
Tel: 0171 229 4408
Topiary frames, wrought iron and wirework furniture, and so on.

CLIFTON NURSERIES
5a Clifton Villas
Little Venice, W9
Tel: 0171 289 6851
Wonderful selection of plants of all shapes and sizes, pots, containers and garden

furniture, as well as a design and garden maintenance service.

MALE ELEGANCE

PAUL SMITH
122 Kensington Park Road, W11
Tel: 0171 727 3553
British fashion designer, Paul Smith's new emporium at

the heart of Notting Hill opened recently in a blaze of publicity.

MUSEUMS AND GALLERIES

LEIGHTON HOUSE
12 Holland Park Road, W14
Tel: 0171 602 3316
The former private home of the famous Pre-Raphaelite painter, Lord Leighton,

Leighton House is renowned for its Arab Hall, a room decorated with a wonderful collection of Iznik tiles.

LINLEY SAMBOURNE HOUSE
18 Stafford Terrace, W8
Tel: 0181 994 1019
Home of Edward Linley Sambourne, a leading cartoonist for the satirical

magazine Punch, the artistic, Victorian interior remains practically unchanged, with original wall decoration and furniture.

THE SAATCHI GALLERY
98a Boundary Road, NW8
Tel: 0171 624 8299
Originally a market garden, this vast gallery was created by architect Max Gordon to

house temporary exhibitions of work from the Saatchi Contemporary Art Collection, which consists of paintings and sculpture of the last twenty-five years. Among the largest collections of works from this period in the world, the gallery is located in St John's Wood, a short distance from the Notting Hill area.

Fulham, Earls Court and Hammersmith

HOTELS

PIPPA POP-INS
430 Fulham Road, SW6
Tel: 0171 385 2458
An hotel especially designed for children without their parents, with windows full of teddy bears and balloons.

RESTAURANTS

ALOUNAK
10 Russell Gardens, W14
Tel: 0171 603 1130
This Persian restaurant started life in a caravan with queues stretching through the car park. Now, in more permanent surroundings, its simple menu is delicious and amazingly cheap.

BALANS WEST
239 Old Brompton Road, SW5
Tel: 0171 244 8838
A modern restaurant with a good atmosphere and fun menu, it is open most of the day and night and proves to be a popular place for Sunday brunch.

BLUE ELEPHANT
4–6 Fulham Broadway, SW6
Tel: 0171 385 6595
An impressive, but expensive Thai restaurant with an

extraordinary tropical setting and consistently delicious food.

CIBO
3 Russell Gardens, W14
Tel: 0171 371 6271
Innovative and delicious Italian cooking compensates for the strange location of this restaurant near Olympia.

THE GATE
51 Queen Caroline Street, W6
Tel: 0181 748 6932
Inventive vegetarian dishes, using only organic ingredients, have made this restaurant very popular. There is a candlelit courtyard in the summer months.

MAO TAI
58 New King's Road, SW6
Tel: 0171 731 2520
Modern surroundings and delicious, well-flavoured Szechuan Chinese food.

MONTANA
125–129 Dawes Road, SW6
Tel: 0171 385 9500

Apart from one of the best brunch restaurants in London, the trendy ambience and interesting American cuisine during the week is often boosted by serious jazz performances.

MR. WING
242–244 Old Brompton Road, SW5
Tel: 0171 370 4450
Extraordinary jungle decor and romantic private seats, together with good Chinese food, make this restaurant a fun night out.

THE RIVER CAFE
Thames Wharf
Rainville Road, W6
Tel: 0171 381 8824
Inspirational cooking and delicious Italian food continue to win this restaurant the highest praise.

BARS

CAMBIO DE TERCIO
163 Old Brompton Road, SW5
Tel: 0171 244 8970
Fun and stylish tapas bar, which also serves other Spanish dishes.

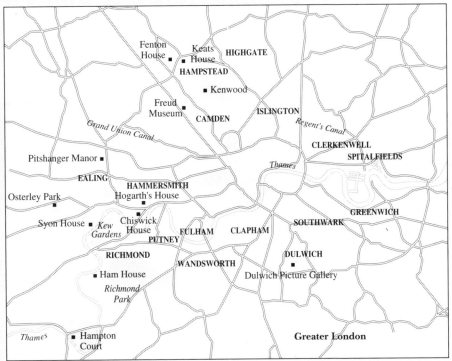

PUBS

ANGLESEA ARMS
35 Wingate Road, W6
0181 749 1291
This trendy pub located in Brackenbury Village serves good and inexpensive modern British food.

THE BRACKENBURY
129–131 Brackenbury Rd, W6
Tel: 0181 748 0107
Serving modern British food, this Shepherd's Bush pub remains a consistent favourite for its atmosphere and menu.

COME THE REVOLUTION
541 King's Road, SW6
Tel: 0171 371 7185
Friendly atmosphere and loud music with a giant fireplace running the length of one wall and a large garden given over to barbecues at the weekend.

THE DOVE
19 Upper Mall, W6
Tel: 0181 748 5405
A riverside pub close to Hammersmith Bridge, famous for its Sunday lunch. During the week Thai food is the order of the day.

FOX & PHEASANT
1 Billing Road, SW10
Tel: 0171 352 2943
In a residential backwater this countrified pub is located just off the Fulham Road. Its white-washed façade is decorated with hanging baskets of flowers, and there is a small courtyard garden to enjoy a beer at the back.

JIM THOMPSON'S
617 King's Road, SW6
Tel: 0171 731 0999
A lively bar at the front of this pub hides a restaurant which is decked out like a Far Eastern bazaar. Thai food is the speciality at this popular meeting place for many who visit the plethora of antique shops at this end of the King's Road.

THE PEN
51 Parson's Green Lane, SW6
Tel: 0171 371 8517
An intimate first-floor dining room above this trendy pub serves good modern British food.

COFFEE BARS

TROUBADOR
265 Old Brompton Road, SW5
An eccentric coffee house in Earl's Court with a Bohemian clientele. A simple menu and a chance to catch up on the papers or play chess.

ANTIQUE SHOPS AND DEALERS

DECORATIVE LIVING
55 New King's Road, SW6
Tel: 0171 736 5623
European, colonial and ethnic furniture and decorative items plus pieces of their own design.

GEORGE SHERLOCK
588 King's Road, SW6
Tel: 0171 736 3955
Decorative furniture, mirrors, bookcases and desks.

GUINEVERE
574–580 King's Road, SW6
Tel: 0171 736 2917
A wonderful Aladdin's Cave of antiques with a large selection of seventeenth- to nineteenth-century continental furniture and objets.

I. & J. L. BROWN
632–636 King's Road, SW6
Tel: 0171 736 4141
French provincial and country furniture and pottery.

JUDY GREENWOOD
657 Fulham Road, SW6
Tel: 0171 736 6037
French beds and a large stock of plain and patchwork antique quilts.

MARK MAYNARD
651 Fulham Road, SW6
Tel: 0171 731 3533
Affordable painted cupboards, armchairs and other furniture.

NICOLE FABRE
592 King's Road, SW6
Tel: 0171 384 3112
Eighteenth- and nineteenth-century French textiles and provincial furniture.

ROBERT BARLEY ANTIQUES
48 Fulham High Street, SW6
Tel: 0171 736 4429
Unusual precious objects dating from 2000 BC to 1940.

RUPERT CAVENDISH
610 King's Road, SW6
Tel: 0171 731 7041
Early and late nineteenth-century Biedermeier, Empire and Russian furniture among others.

SYLVIA NAPIER
554 King's Road, SW6
Tel: 0171 371 5881
Eclectic mix of European and oriental antiques.

Chelsea, South Kensington and Knightsbridge

HOTELS

BAILEY'S
140 Gloucester Road, SW7
Tel: 0171 373 6000
One of the larger hotels in this area, Bailey's benefits from its proximity to the Bombay Brasserie, still one of London's finest Indian restaurants.

BLAKE'S
33 Roland Gardens, SW7
Tel: 0171 370 6701
Occupying several buildings in this residential street, Blake's was designed by Anouska Hempel.
Each of its rooms has a unique look and there is a fashionable bar and restaurant in the basement.

THE CAPITAL
22–24 Basil Street, SW3
Tel: 0171 589 5171
Exclusive hotel of forty-eight rooms located close to Harrods and the shops of Sloane Street with an excellent restaurant specialising in modern French cuisine.

CLIVEDEN TOWN HOUSE
24–26 Cadogan Gardens, SW3
Tel: 0171 730 6466
A red-brick Victorian end-of-terrace building overlooking a classic garden square and located just off Sloane Square. Meals are limited to room service only, but there are numerous local restaurants to choose from.

EGERTON HOUSE
17–19 Egerton Terrace, SW3
Tel: 0171 589 2412
Close neighbour to The Franklin, and under the same ownership, this hotel is a smaller version with only twenty-nine rooms.

ELEVEN CADOGAN GARDENS
11 Cadogan Gardens, SW3
Tel: 0171 730 7000
A discreet address in the heart of residential Knightsbridge which serves a wonderful English tea, although other meals are limited to room service.

FIVE SUMNER PLACE
5 Sumner Place, SW7
Tel: 0171 584 7586
A small bed & breakfast of thirteen rooms in this residential street off the Old Brompton Road at the heart of South Kensington, it was recently voted London's best B & B.

THE FRANKLIN
28 Egerton Gardens, SW3
Tel: 0171 584 5533
Another Victorian red-brick townhouse located in a quiet residential street just off the Brompton Road and close to the Victoria & Albert Museum. Room service only.

L'HOTEL
28 Basil Street, SW3
Tel: 0171 589 6286
Owned by The Capital Hotel next door, this charming bed and breakfast also benefits

from a separate basement restaurant, the Metro Bar.

MANDARIN ORIENTAL HYDE PARK
66 Knightsbridge, SW1
Tel: 0171 235 2000
A Knightsbridge landmark, this large red-brick Victorian hotel is located opposite Harvey Nichols and backs onto the peace and tranquility of Hyde Park.

THE PELHAM
15 Cromwell Place, SW7
Tel: 0171 589 8288
Located at the centre of South Kensington, close to the big museums and a short walk from Hyde Park, this hotel offers a variety of designer-decorated rooms and its own restaurant.

SYDNEY HOUSE
9–11 Sydney Street, SW3
Tel: 0171 376 7711
A terraced Victorian town-house just off the South Kensington end of the Fulham Road, ideally situated for shopping in both the King's Road and Fulham Road.

RESTAURANTS

AUBERGINE
11 Park Walk, SW10
Tel: 0171 352 3449
The delicious modern French cuisine produced by this restaurant ensures that it is almost impossible to book a table less than several weeks in advance.

BANGKOK
9 Bute Street, SW7
Tel: 0171 584 8529
The restaurant is minimally furnished for basic comfort, but the authentic Thai food is consistently good and prepared under the eye of the customer.

BERSAGLIERA
372 King's Road, SW3

Tel: 0171 352 5993
A cheap and cheerful pizza and pasta restaurant, with reputedly the best garlic bread in London.

BIBENDUM OYSTER BAR
81 Fulham Road, SW3
Tel: 0171 589 1480
Located at the ground-floor entrance to the Conran Shop in the Michelin Building at trendy Brompton Cross, the fish, seafood and oysters served here continue to earn great praise from local devotees.

BISTROT 190
189–190 Queen's Gate, SW7
Tel: 0171 581 5666
An informal brasserie within the Gore Hotel, located a short distance from the Royal Albert Hall. Brunch and an interesting selection of Mediterranean dishes makes it a popular restaurant on a first-come-first-served basis. They do not take bookings.

BLUEBIRD
350 King's Road, SW3
Tel: 0171 559 1000
Not just a restaurant, but an emporium, with a cafe, supermarket, florist and housewares shop all in the same complex. Built by Terence Conran on the site of a former ambulance garage this is now one of the places to be seen on the King's Road.

BOMBAY BRASSERIE
Courtfield Close
Gloucester Road, SW7
Tel: 0171 370 4040
Renowned Indian restaurant with a huge conservatory in which the atmosphere epitomises the last days of the Raj. The food is generally excellent, with a buffet lunch on Sundays.

LA BRASSERIE
272 Brompton Road, SW3

Tel: 0171 584 1668
In addition to its long-standing popularity as a good place to rendezvous during a hectic day's shopping, Sunday brunch is adding to the clientele of this restaurant.

THE CANTEEN
Chelsea Harbour, SW10
Tel: 0171 351 7330
Good modern British food continues to bring in the custom, despite its location out on a limb in the Chelsea Harbour complex.

CHELSEA BUN DINER
9a Lamont Road, SW10
Tel: 0171 352 3635
At this curious combination of American diner/British transport cafe, English break-fast is served all day, together with a good choice of vegetarian meals.

THE ENTERPRISE
35 Walton Street, SW3
Tel: 0171 584 3148
A favourite stand-by for lunch among the interior designers and ladies who frequent the shops along Walton Street. A converted pub, it has become a fashion-able location for both lunch and dinner.

FIFTH FLOOR AT HARVEY NICHOLS
Knightsbridge, SW1
Tel: 0171 823 1839
Not to be confused with the restaurant, this all-day cafe at the top of Harvey Nichols offers easy food and a break from the shopping.

JOE'S CAFE
126 Draycott Avenue, SW3
Tel: 0171 225 2217
Another restaurant for shoppers. Located in Bromp-ton Cross, it serves modern British food and is gaining a reputation for Sunday brunch.

HOUSEHOLD SHOPS

The English obsession with buying things for the home finds outlets in London to satisfy every requirement.

The Conran Shop
81 Fulham Road, SW3
Tel: 0171 589 7401

Divertimenti
139 Fulham Road, SW3
Tel: 0171 581 8065

Graham & Greene
4 & 7 Elgin Crescent, W11
Tel: 0171 727 4594

The Holding Company
245 King's Road, SW3
Tel: 0171 352 1600

Jerry's Home Store
163 Fulham Road, SW3
Tel: 0171 581 0909

Muji
157 Kensington High Street, W8
Tel: 0171 376 2484

The Source
26 Kensington High Street, W8
Tel: 0171 937 2626

MONA LISA
417 King's Road, SW10
Tel: 0171 376 5447
A transport cafe in World's End, it offers a combination of cheap Italian dishes and traditional British fry-ups in a simple atmosphere whose appeal is universal.

PASHA
1 Gloucester Road, SW7
Tel: 0171 589 7969
Delicious, light Moroccan cuisine, served by waiters in full costume in an atmo-spheric setting.

PIZZA ON THE PARK
11 Knightsbridge, SW1
Tel: 0171 235 5273
A huge restaurant right near Hyde Park Corner which serves decent pizzas as well as a great breakfast. Jazz goes on regularly in the basement for a substantial extra charge.

SAN LORENZO
22 Beauchamp Place, SW3
Tel: 0171 584 1074
Italian trattoria for the "in-crowd" where chosen cus-tomers are greeted as if they were members of an elite club and outsiders made to feel unwelcome.

LA TANTE CLAIRE
68–69 Royal Hospital Road,

SW3
Tel: 0171 352 6045
Still considered to be one of the best of the London restaurants, with wonderful French cooking and a great value lunch menu.

T'SU
118 Draycott Avenue, SW3
Tel: 0171 584 5522
A sushi conveyor-belt cafe with a modern setting on the corner of Walton Street, attracting a steady stream of shoppers.

BARS

ALBERO & GRANA TAPAS BAR
89 Sloane Avenue, SW3
Tel: 0171 225 1048
A stylish bar serving afford-able light food makes an entertaining rendezvous.

BAR AT 190
190 Queen's Gate, SW7
Tel: 0171 581 5666
A dark wood-panelled bar furnished with comfortable sofas and armchairs forms part of The Gore Hotel, which also has a good restau-rant and a separate bistro.

CACTUS BLUE
86 Fulham Road, SW3
Tel: 0171 823 7858
The combination of modern

and fun decor with Latin-American inspired food and a casual atmosphere make this an interesting bar/restaurant for a cool night out.

THE CRESCENT
99 Fulham Road, SW3
Tel: 0171 225 2244
Fashionably located near Brompton Cross, The Crescent has a fantastic wine list offering over two hundred different wines by the glass.

FOXTROT OSCAR
79 Royal Hospital Road, SW3
Tel: 0171 352 7179
A wine-bar/diner near the Royal Hospital and Chelsea Physic Garden, with a friendly atmosphere.

LE METRO
28 Basil Street, SW3
Tel: 0171 589 6286
A short distance from Harrods and Harvey Nichols, this all-day wine bar next to The Capital Hotel has a wonderful selection of wines by the glass, together with modern British food.

WINE GALLERY
49 Hollywood Road, SW10
Tel: 0171 352 7572
The wine here is served at merchant prices, giving this wine bar the edge on some of its neighbours. A slightly predictable interior is helped considerably in summer by a courtyard garden.

PUBS

CHELSEA RAM
32 Burnaby Street, SW10
Tel: 0171 351 4008
Located not far from Lot's Road Auction House, where many Londoners empty or furnish their houses, this pub offers good British cooking in a packed atmosphere.

COOPERS ARMS
87 Flood Street, SW3
Tel: 0171 376 3120
One of the genre of updated pubs, genuine home-prepared food is served here in comfortable surroundings.

THE CROSS KEYS
1 Lawrence Street, SW3
Tel: 0171 349 9111
A stylish pub conversion incorporates a conservatory into its design, with standard British pub food on offer.

FRONT PAGE
35 Old Church Street, SW3
Tel: 0171 352 2908
Old Chelsea pub located between the King's Road and the Embankment that serves good food in a friendly setting.

DELICATESSENS, COFFEE AND JUICE BARS

BAKER & SPICE
46 Walton Street, SW3
Tel: 0171 589 4734
The heart of every village is the bakery, and in Chelsea Baker & Spice have a reputation which brings customers from far and wide to sample their bread, patisseries and other delectables.

CAFFE NERO
66 Old Brompton Road, SW7
Tel: 0171 589 1760
Cool, clean and stainless steel, with delicious coffee and a good range of break-fast pastries baked on the premises, supplemented at lunchtime with pizzas and rolls.

THE FIFTH FLOOR AT HARVEY NICHOLS
67 Brompton Road, SW3
Tel: 0171 584 0011
Exotic goods are beautifully displayed on metal shelves, giving a modern feel to this

high class supermarket on the top floor of the fashionable Knightsbridge store.

FINNS
4 Elystan Street, SW3
Tel: 0171 225 0733
Quite simply, the best sandwiches in London!

THE FOOD HALL AT HARRODS
Knightsbridge, SW1
Tel: 0171 730 1234
Eighteen different departments, in the famous Art Deco tiled halls, sell speciality teas, freshly ground coffee, 116 types of bread, chocolates, patisseries, fresh fish, meat, cheese, and more—all beautifully displayed. It is still an experience to shop at Harrods but go early to avoid the crowds.

> ## TEA AT THE CHELSEA PHYSIC GARDEN
> Disregard the schoolroom style of the surroundings and take advantage of the best tea in London. After an educational potter around the Chelsea Physic Garden, tea is served in a large building near the outer wall. Tables literally groan with plates of home-made cakes and biscuits, meringues, strawberries and cream and other delights, washed down with gallons of good, strong tea. Not to be missed.

KING'S ROAD CAFE
206 King's Road, SW3
Tel: 0171 351 664
Cafe located on the first floor of Habitat that offers reasonably priced meals, coffee and cakes as a good shopping break.

LUIGI'S DELICATESSEN
349 Fulham Road, SW10
Tel: 0171 352 7739
An institution on the Fulham Road, this Italian delicatessen serves delicious cheese, ham, fresh pasta and the like to an enthusiastic clientele.

PATISSERIE VALERIE
215 Brompton Road, SW3
Tel: 0171 823 9971
Beautifully decorated, and offering delicious tea, coffee and a plethora of mouth-watering cakes and pastries, the cafe is located conveniently close to the many large museums at this end of South Kensington.

PICASSO
127 King's Road, SW3
Tel: 0171 352 4921
Shiny Harley-Davidson motorbikes are parked on the pavement outside this coffee house, where the clientele come to people-watch over a cappuccino.

PARTRIDGES OF SLOANE STREET
132 Sloane Street, SW1
Tel: 0171 730 0651
A vast double-fronted delicatessen with every conceivable delicacy to tempt even the most fastidious palate.

LA PICENA
5 Walton Street, SW3
Tel: 0171 584 6573
A tiny delicatessen on this street of restaurants and interior design shops, it provides a demanding clientele with fresh Italian fare.

RAISON D'ETRE
18 Bute Street, SW7
Tel: 0171 584 5008
It seems natural to find a French café close to the lycée in a street full of French shops. Serves good coffee, sandwiches and pastries.

ANTIQUE SHOPS, DEALERS AND AUCTION HOUSES

ALASDAIR BROWN
24 Chelsea Wharf
15 Lots Road, SW10
Tel: 0171 351 1477
Nineteenth-century Gothic furniture, paintings and objets from Europe and Scandinavia.

ANTIQUARIUS
131–141 King's Road, SW3
Tel: 0171 351 5353
Over 120 specialist dealers in everything imaginable, and all under the one roof, at the heart of the King's Road.

BONHAMS
Montpelier Street, SW7
Tel: 0171 393 3900
A wide range of specialised sales take place at this well-known auction house.

BONHAMS CHELSEA
65–69 Lots Road, SW10
Tel: 0171 393 3999
Less expensive items, from furniture to contemporary art, tend to be auctioned off at this Lots Road branch of Bonhams.

CHRISTIE'S SOUTH KENSINGTON
85 Old Brompton Road, SW7
Tel: 0171 581 7611
Less grand items and collections tend to find their way to this smaller branch of Christie's auction house.

COSKUN & CO. LTD.
56a Walton Street, SW3
Tel: 0171 581 9056
Exhibitions and sales of engravings and screen prints by Andy Warhol, Matisse and Picasso in the comfort and intimate surroundings of Gul Coskun's Chelsea home.

DAVID GILL
60 Fulham Road, SW3
Tel: 0171 589 5946

Twentieth-century and contemporary furniture, including designers, Garouste & Bonetti, Oriel Harwood and Donald Judd.

THE FURNITURE CAVE
533 King's Road, SW10
Tel: 0171 352 4229
The home of a group of independent antique dealers, selling in furniture and objets of all periods and styles.

GORDON WATSON
50 Fulham Road, SW3
Tel: 0171 589 3108
Art deco furniture and accessories of 1920–1940.

JOANNA BOOTH
247 King's Road, SW3
Tel: 0171 352 8998
Sixteenth to eighteenth-century tapestry and antique textiles.

LOTS ROAD AUCTION GALLERIES
71 Lots Road, SW10
Tel: 0171 351 7771
Bonhams direct competitor, the two houses are also neighbours, with auctions on different nights of the week.

O. F. WILSON
3–6 Queens Elm Parade
Old Church Street, SW3
Tel: 0171 352 9554
Eighteenth- and early nineteenth-century furniture, marble and stone fireplaces, mirrors and architectural items.

GARDENING SHOPS AND CENTRES

THE CHELSEA GARDENER
125 Sydney Street, SW3
Tel: 0171 352 5656
A plethora of plants and flowers, garden furniture, books, pots and lighting, together with a garden design and maintenance service, if required.

THE CHELSEA PHYSIC GARDEN
Royal Hospital Road, SW3
Tel: 0171 352 5646
Open to the public from April to October on Sunday and Wednesday afternoons only, the Chelsea Physic Garden is full of fascinating plants and flowers. Cuttings and seeds can be bought from the nursery.

THE CONRAN SHOP
Michelin House
81 Fulham Road, SW3
Tel: 0171 589 7401
Garden furniture, pots and other garden style ornaments. A wonderful selection of cut flowers are sold from an old French Citroën van, parked in front of the store.

MALE ELEGANCE

BERTIE WOOSTER
284 Fulham Road, SW10
Tel: 0171 352 5662
Second-hand clothes

COYS OF KENSINGTON
2–4 Queen's Gate Mews, SW7
Tel: 0171 584 7444
The double-fronted glass windows of this tiny mews showroom are filled with the vintage cars most people can only dream about–from a red Ferrari, jaunty roadster, or sleek Alvis to a venerable Rolls Royce.

HACKETT'S
136 Sloane Street, SW1
Tel: 0171 730 3331

PAPYRUS
48 Fulham Road, SW3

Tel: 0171 584 8022
A family business which specialises in luxury leather goods, personalised stationery and other unusual gifts.

STEINBERG & TOLKEIN
193 King's Road, SW3
Tel: 0171 376 3660

VOYAGE
175 Fulham Road, SW3
Tel: 0171 352 8611
Wonderfully exotic and eclectic clothes for men, with a shop for women a few steps further down the Fulham Road.

MUSEUMS

CARLYLE HOUSE
24 Cheyne Row, SW3
Tel: 0171 352 7087
Former home of the Victorian writer and historian Thomas Carlyle, the house is now managed by the National Trust and maintained very much as it would have been in Carlyle's day (see page 178).

OLD BATTERSEA HOUSE
30 Vicarage Crescent, SW11
Tel: 0181 871 7037

Not strictly Chelsea, but a short hop south of the river, Old Battersea House is a private home which houses the Forbes' collection of early Victorian paintings, together with the Pre-Raphaelite paintings and lustreware belonging to the De Morgan Foundation. By appointment only on Wednesday afternoons (see page 181).

THE SERPENTINE GALLERY
Kensington Gardens, SW7
Tel: 0171 823 9727
Temporary exhibitions of contemporary art take place in this former Victorian tea pavilion on the edge of Kensington Gardens.

VICTORIA & ALBERT MUSEUM
Cromwell Road
South Kensington, SW7
Tel: 0171 938 8441
The largest and most famous decorative arts museum in the world. In addition to its wonderful permanent exhibitions, the V & A also has exhibitions linked with the fashion world and costume collections.

Belgravia, Victoria and Pimlico

HOTELS

THE BERKELEY
Wilton Place, SW1
Tel: 0171 235 6000
One of the stable of Savoy hotels, The Berkeley is popular with shoppers and business executives alike. One of its many attractions, the swimming pool at the top of the hotel has a sliding roof and wonderful views over Hyde Park.

THE GORING
22 Beeston Place, SW1
Tel: 0171396 9000
A reliable hotel with a quiet private garden, located in a side street just behind Buckingham Palace.

THE HALKIN
5 Halkin Street, SW1
Tel: 0171 333 1000
Located just off Belgrave Square, the hotel has an Italian influence,

in both its architecture and the Armani uniforms worn by its staff.

THE LANESBOROUGH
1 Lanesborough Place, SW1
Tel: 0171 259 5599
Situated at Hyde Park Corner, overlooking Apsley House and the gardens of Hyde Park, this five-star hotel is at the centre of the action.

RUBENS
39–41 Buckingham Palace Road, SW1
Tel: 0171 834 6600
Located opposite the Royal Mews at the rear of Buckingham Palace, this hotel is wonderfully central.

ST JAMES COURT
45 Buckingham Gate, SW1
Tel: 0171 834 6655
This large hotel located between Victoria and Buck-

ingham Palace is well-known for its Chinese restaurant.

RESTAURANTS

AL BUSTAN
27 Motcomb Street, SW1
Tel: 0171 235 8277
Large portions of good Lebanese food in discreet surroundings, ideal for a quiet night out.

COMO LARIO
22 Holbein Place, SW1
Tel: 0171 730 2954
Friendly and always crowded
trattoria serving typical
Italian food.

HUNAN
51 Pimlico Road, SW1
Tel: 0171 730 5712
Spicy and original Chinese
food is guaranteed at this
long-standing favourite near
Pimlico Green.

KEN LO'S MEMORIES
67–69 Ebury Street, SW1
Tel: 0171 730 7734
Superb cooking with distinctive flavours keeps an enthusiastic following for
this quiet and simple
Chinese restaurant.

MARABEL'S
16 St Barnabas Street, SW1
Tel: 0171 730 5550
Despite its not very London
decor, this newly opened
restaurant in Pimlico is recommended for its delicious
Italian/French food–
at least three different
risottos are available.

OLIVETO
49 Elizabeth Street, SW1
Tel: 0171 730 0074
Cool, stylish and affordable
Italian restaurant serving
good pizza and pasta.

OLIVO
21 Eccleston Street, SW1
Tel: 0171 730 2505
Sardinian cuisine and an
interesting menu inter-
spersed with weekly specials
in jolly blue and yellow
surroundings make this a
popular restaurant.

ORIEL
50–51 Sloane Square, SW1
Tel: 0171 730 2804
This brasserie located
right on the square next
to the Royal Court Theatre
is a useful meeting point
at the end of a day's

shopping. It also has a
reputation for very
good breakfast.

LA POULE AU POT
231 Ebury Street, SW1
Tel: 0171 730 7763
This candle-lit, romantic
restaurant is an old favourite
more for its setting than the
French cuisine.

SEAFRESH
80–81 Wilton Road, SW1
Tel: 0171 828 0747
As the name suggests,
the attraction of this traditional fish & chips style
restaurant is the superb
fish, together with an
acceptable wine list.

**TATE GALLERY
RESTAURANT**
Millbank, SW1
Tel: 0171 887 8877
Good affordable wines,
from a list rated the best in

London, and the famous
Whistler murals make this
restaurant a popular meeting
place for lunch or afternoon
tea. It is closed evenings.

UNO
1 Denbigh Street, SW1
Tel: 0171 834 1001
Another of the area's fun
Italian restaurants to add to
the list of those specialising
in pizza and pasta.

VONG (at The Berkeley)
Wilton Place, SW1
Tel: 0171 235 1010
French–Thai cuisine in a
modern setting has made
this a very popular spot.

ZAFFERANO
15 Lowndes Street, SW1
Tel: 0171 235 5800
A stylish Italian restaurant
that serves deliciously
different food in a
sophisticated setting.

FLORISTS

The English have always
had a reputation for
flower-arranging, their
interiors filled with fresh
blooms throughout the year.
London has a variety of
wonderful florists and
flower shops.
In addition, there are stalls
on practically every street
corner, their banks of
colour bright against the
brick façades of buildings,
the mixed scent heavy
on the air.

Basia Zarzycka
135 King's Road, SW3
Tel: 351 7276

The Flower Van
Michelin Building
81 Fulham Road, SW3
Tel: 0171 589 1852

Harper & Tom's Flowers
73 Clarendon Road, W11
Tel: 0171 792 8510

Jane Packer
56 James Street, W1
Tel: 0171 935 2673

Kenneth Turner
125 Mount Street, W1
Tel: 0171 355 3880

Moyses Stevens
157–158 Sloane Street, SW1
Tel: 0171 259 9303

Paula Pryke Flowers
20 Penton Street, N1
Tel: 0171 837 7336

Pulbrook & Gould
127 Sloane Street, SW1
Tel: 0171 730 0030

Wild at Heart
Turquoise Island
222 Westbourne Grove, W11
Tel: 0171 727 3095
another branch at:
49a Ledbury Road, W11

Woodhams
60 Ledbury Road, W11
Tel: 0171 243 3141

BARS

BOISDALE
15 Eccleston Street, SW1
Tel: 0171 730 6922
There is a "clubby" atmo-
sphere in this modern
British wine bar/restaurant.
It also boasts the largest
collection of whiskies in
London, an extensive wine
list and good bar snacks.

EBURY STREET WINE BAR
139 Ebury Street, SW1
Tel: 0171 730 5447
Modern British food,
together with a traditional
wine-bar atmosphere,
prolong this bar's popularity.

THE LIBRARY
The Lanesborough, SW1
Tel: 0171 259 5599
The high-ceilinged Library
Bar is the place to go for the
start of a evening out. With a
wide variety of cocktails and
a spirits menu offering forty
whiskies, live music is
provided by a flamboyant
pianist.

PIMLICO WINE VAULTS
19–22 Upper Tachbrook
Street, SW1
Tel: 0171 834 7429
A traditional basement wine
bar which makes up for its
dated ambience by a list of
over eighty wines and good
bar food.

TILES
36 Buckingham Palace Road,
SW1
Tel: 0171 834 7761
Tiles specialises in particularly trendy wines from Aus-
tralia, New Zealand, Chile
and California, along with a
few other unexpected places,
which make up a wine list of
around fifty varieties.

PUBS

THE ANTELOPE
22–24 Eaton Terrace, SW1
Tel: 0171 730 7781

Original and well-cared for,
this old-fashioned pub is
popular with the locals.

THE GRENADIER
18 Wilton Row, SW1
Tel: 0171 235 3074
A tourist attraction in the
summer, this small pub
tucked away in a Belgrave
mews serves delicious
sausages as well as
raditional pub fare.

DELICATESSENS, COFFEE AND JUICE BARS

CITY HARVEST
38 Buckingham Palace Road,
SW1
Tel: 0171 630 9781
Close to Buckingham Palace
and very much on the route
of the weary tourist, the City
Harvest offers an oasis for
the footsore thanks to its
good food and delicious
coffee.

HAMLET COFFEE SHOP
12 Artillery Row, SW1
Tel: 0171 828 9040
Breakfast, sandwiches or
home-made soup and good
coffee keep a loyal clientele
coming back for more.

THE WELL
2 Eccleston Place, SW1
Tel: 0171 730 7303
A short distance from
Victoria Station, The Well is
a haven of tranquility. Dishes
are freshly prepared and
there is a choice of hand-
made cakes, scones and
biscuits.

ANTIQUE SHOPS

ANTIQUUS
90/92 Pimlico Road, SW1
Tel: 0171 730 8691
European textiles, furniture
and glass.

CARLTON HOBBS
46 Pimlico Road, SW1
Tel: 0171 730 3640

Museum-quality English and Continental furniture and works of art.

CHRISTOPER GIBBS
3 Dove Walk
Pimlico Road,
SW1
Tel: 0171 730 8200
Recently moved from Vigo Street, Christopher Gibbs specialises in paintings of all periods, decorative furniture and other works of art
(see page 100).

CHRISTOPHER HODSOLL LTD.
91 Pimlico Road,
SW1
Tel: 0171 730 3370
Eighteenth- and nineteenth-century English country-house furniture, antiques and works of art.

DAVID LINLEY FURNITURE LTD.
60 Pimlico Road, SW1
Tel: 0171 730 7300
"Couture" furniture manufactured by a group of specialist workshops, the style is inspired by elements of architectural and classical detail.

HERAZ
2 Halkin Arcade, SW1
Tel: 0171 245 9497
Specialists in seventeenth- to nineteenth-century tapestry cushions, antique carpets and tapestries.

HERMITAGE ANTIQUES
97 Pimlico Road,
SW1
Tel: 0171 730 1973
Early nineteenth-century Biedermeier, Empire and Russian furniture, among others.

JOSS GRAHAM ORIENTAL TEXTILES
10 Eccleston Street, SW1
Tel: 0171 730 4370
New and antique textiles from India, Central Asia and the Middle and Far East, together with a fine selection of kilims.

MCCED
8 Holbein Place, SW1
Tel: 0171 730 4025
Nineteenth-century architectural furniture, objects and lighting.

MCCLENAGHAN
69 Pimlico Road, SW1
Tel: 0171 730 4187
Grand antiques and objects.

ROGIER ANTIQUES
20a Pimlico Road, SW1
Tel: 0171 823 4780
Mainly French, but some

Continental decorative antiques.

GARDENING SHOPS AND CENTRES

MARSTON & LANGINGER
192 Ebury Street, SW1
Tel: 0171 824 8818
Specialists in conservatory design, they sell ranges of wooden and wicker garden furniture, pots, and so on.

MALE ELEGANCE

CONNOLLY
32 Grosvenor Crescent Mews, SW1
Tel: 0171 235 3883
A luxury leather company, which manufactures wonderful luggage and accessories, in addition to providing the upholstery for many luxury cars.

FRANK SMYTHSON LTD.
132 Sloane Street, SW1
Tel: 0171 730 5520
Smythson's reputation for leather-bound diaries and expensive stationery continues.

MUSEUMS

TATE GALLERY
Millbank, SW1
Tel: 0171 887 8000
Temporary and permanent exhibitions of contemporary modern art, a permanent collection of British painting from sixteenth century to 1900 which includes the Turner Bequest and the Pre-Raphaelites. The Tate also houses the national collection of twentieth-century painting and sculpture.

St. James's, Mayfair and the West End

HOTELS

22 JERMYN STREET
22 Jermyn Street, SW1
Tel: 0171 734 2353
A private hotel of eighteen rooms and five suites which has been in the same family for three generations, the emphasis here is on personal service. It is located in the centre of St James's and surrounded by many of the shops which specialise in male elegance.

BROWN'S
30 Albemarle Street, W1
Tel: 0171 493 6020
Recently refurbished, Brown's continues to live on its long established reputation for traditional English service. It has entrances in both Albemarle and Dover

Streets, which can be useful, and it is still a favourite place for business breakfasts and afternoon tea.

CLARIDGE'S
Brook Street, W1
Tel: 0171 629 8860
High society's favourite hotel, Claridge's still epitomises discretion and service. Its Art Deco interior and magnificent lobby, the frock-coated waiters and the air of tranquility which pervades, continue to keep it high on the list of best hotels in London.

CONNAUGHT
Carlos Place, W1
Tel: 0171 491 0668
The Connaught has always been popular with those traditionalists who like its

grand, club-like atmosphere. The restaurant is still rated as outstanding and regarded as a treat.

DORCHESTER
Park Lane, W1
Tel: 0171 629 8888
One of London's best-known hotels, it has several good restaurants and a world-wide reputation.

DUKES
35 St James's Place, SW1
Tel: 0171 491 4840
A red-brick Victorian townhouse located in a discreet courtyard in St James's, Dukes has a clubby atmosphere and a good bar.

DURRANTS
26–32 George Street, W1
Tel: 0171 935 8131

Family-run hotel with a discreet charm, located just off Baker Street.

FORTY-SEVEN PARK STREET
47 Park Street, W1
Tel: 0171 491 7282
Just off Park Lane, furnished like an English country hotel, this discreet hotel benefits from its association with the French restaurant, Le Gavroche, which also provides the room-service menu.

FOUR SEASONS
Hamilton Place
Park Lane, W1
Tel: 0171 734 8000
Another of the five-star hotels located near Hyde Park with good views and restaurants to match.

Lunch is particularly good value.

HAZLITT'S
6 Frith Street, W1
Tel: 0171 434 1771
Hazlitt's is located in the heart of Soho, close to the theatres and major West End cinemas and the centre of London's night life.

THE LEONARD
15 Seymour Street,
W1
Tel: 0171 935 2010
A townhouse hotel with 31 rooms, The Leonard is located conveniently just off Oxford Street and within walking distance of The Wallace Collection. It has a cafe bar and a limited evening menu.

LE MERIDIEN PICCADILLY
21 Piccadilly, W1
Tel: 0171 734 8000
Just off Piccadilly Circus,
this hotel is in the centre
of London's West End and
theatreland and also conveniently located for shopping
in Regent Street and the
Haymarket.

THE METROPOLITAN
19 Old Park Lane, W1
Tel: 0171 447 4747
Marketed as the only really
trendy hotel in London,
The Metropolitan has a stark
almost minimalist interior, a
remarkable restaurant,
Nobu, and a particlarly
trendy bar, combined with a
spectacular view of Hyde
Park from the bedrooms
on the Park Lane side of
the hotel.

THE RITZ
150 Piccadilly, W1
Tel: 0171 493 8181
The name has been long
associated with grandeur and
glamour and the decoration
of The Ritz in London continues to emphasise this
distinction. It remains a
favourite meeting place.

STAFFORD
16–18 St James's Place,
SW1
Tel: 0171 493 0111
A stone's throw from Dukes
and located in an equally
quiet backwater, The
Stafford continues to
maintain a reputation for
reliable and discreet service.

RESTAURANTS

AL HAMRA
31–33 Shepherd Market,
W1
Tel: 0171 493 1954
Shepherd Market is a lively
area, particularly at night,
and this consistently good
Lebanese restaurant spills
out onto the pavement
during the summer.

ANDREW EDMUNDS
46 Lexington Street, W1
Tel: 0171 437 5708
Simple, but imaginative,
modern British food at
affordable prices with an
inexpensive wine list, served
in a wonderful, candle-lit
atmosphere.

BOUDIN BLANC
5 Trebeck Street, W1
Tel: 0171 499 3292
Just off Curzon Street and
near the lively Shepherd
Market, this French bistro
offers reliable food in a cosy,
if basic, atmosphere.

LE CAPRICE
Arlington House
Arlington Street, SW1
Tel: 0171 629 2239
This modern brasserie in St
James's, situated just behind
The Ritz, serves delicious
food and offers a chance to
people-watch if you are lucky
enough to get a table.

COAST
26b Albemarle Street, W1
Tel: 0171 495 5999
Spartan, trendy restaurant in
the heart of Mayfair, which
opened a couple of years ago
to great publicity. The modern British cuisine attracts
the customers more than the
over-designed interior.

THE CRITERION
Piccadilly Circus, W1
Tel: 0171 930 0488
Regarded as the most suc-
cessful of the several restaurants belonging to Marco
Pierre White, The Criterion
is probably the most beautiful room in London. It is
decorated in a neo-Byzantine
style with tiny coloured tiles.

DORCHESTER ORIENTAL
Park Lane, W1
Tel: 0171 317 6328
Dubbed the capital's grandest oriental, this Chinese
restaurant at The Dorchester
is probably also the most

expensive, although the food
would seem to justify the
price.

GAY HUSSAR
2 Greek Street, W1
Tel: 0171 437 0973
This famously romantic Hun-
garian restaurant has been a
favourite London institution
for years and continues in
the same tradition.

KASPIA
18–18a Bruton Place, W1
Tel: 0171 493 2612
Located in a tiny mews,
Kaspia specialises in caviar.
It has a delicious, if short,
menu.

MIRABELLE
56 Curzon Street, W1
Tel.: 0171 499 4636
Celebrity chef Marco Pierre
White's latest and by all
accounts most successful
restaurant to date, serving
generous proportions of delicious French food at a reasonable price in a stylish
1930s setting.

MITSUKOSHI
14–16 Regent Street, SW1
Tel: 0171 930 0317
Considered to be the best
Japanese restaurant in London, it is praised particularly
for its very fresh sushi.

MOMO
25 Heddon Street, W1
Tel: 0171 434 4040
Momo, located just off
Regent Street, has been *the*
place to be seen this year,
with a very trendy basement
bar. The restaurant serves
spicy Moroccan food.

NOBU
Metropolitan Hotel
Old Park Lane, W1
Tel: 0171 447 4747
The Metropolitan has always
been inundated with models
and people from the fashion
world and Matsuhisa Nobu's
mix of Japanese/South

American cuisine was an
instant success.

L'ORANGER
5 St James's Street, SW1
Tel: 0171 839 3774
Due to its sophisticated
French cooking and excel-
lent service in a traditional
setting with a charming conservatory, l'Oranger is now
considered to be one of the
best restaurants in town.

QUAGLINO'S
16 Bury Street, W1
Tel: 0171 930 6767
This buzzing and glamorous
brasserie in the heart of St
James's is considered to be
the nicest of Sir Terence
Conran's numerous large
restaurants. The menu
concentrates on grills
and seafood.

SARTORIA
20 Savile Row, W1
Tel: 0171 534 7000
Conran's latest restaurant to
open has proved an instant
success with excellent Italian
cuisine. Half-finished suits
hanging in frames around
the walls and other decorative motives reflect the
restaurant's location in Savile
Row, the heart of London's
tailoring industry.

SOTHEBY'S CAFE
34 New Bond Street, W1
Tel: 0171 408 5077
Situated off the foyer of
Sotheby's auction house, the
cafe, which opened last year,
has gained a reputation for a
good light lunch. It also
serves breakfast and tea
while encouraging would-be
bidders to stay in-house.

SRI SIAM
16 Old Compton Street, W1
Tel: 0171 434 3544
Considered to be one of the
top oriental restaurants in
London, Sri Siam serves
beautifully presented
Thai food.

SUNTORY
72 St James's Street, SW1
Tel: 0171 409 0201
London's longest established
Japanese restaurant continues to serve good, beautifully
presented food.

TAMARIND
20 Queen Street, W1
Tel: 0171 629 3561
Unusual nouvelle Indian
cuisine is served in this
basement restaurant just off
Berkeley Square in a sophisticated, tranquil atmosphere.

VENDOME
20 Dover Street, W1
Tel: 0171 629 5417
The decor of this intimate
Mayfair restaurant is elegant
and dramatic. Modern
British cuisine and attentive
service (see page 197).

YO! SUSHI
52–53 Poland Street, W1
Tel: 0171 287 0443
Food and drinks delivered by
robot or on conveyor belt in
a space-age environment are
the main attractions.

BARS

ATLANTIC BAR & GRILL
20 Glasshouse Street, SW1
Tel: 0171 734 4888
This vast and glamorous
basement with a classical/Art
Deco interior near Piccadilly
Circus has effectively three
bars. The main bar has
waiter service in the seated
areas; Dick's Bar has a more
intimate feel and cocktails
are served; while the circular
Chez Cup is available for
private hire.

CAFE DE PARIS
3 Coventry Street, W1
Tel: 0171 734 7700
This cool bar/restaurant is a
conversion of the famous
1930s nightclub. A large
selection of cocktails in very
chic surroundings makes for
quite an experience.

DOVER STREET WINE BAR

8–10 Dover Street, W1
Tel: 0171 629 9813
This Mayfair cellar with its black-and-white interior seems to be one of the few places where you can still eat and have a boogie at the same time. It is a jazz bar which takes itself very seriously.

FLUTES WINE BAR

61 Goodge Street, W1
Tel: 0171 637 0177
A long thin basement and a classic wine-bar decor, with romantic lighting and a small restaurant area, nearly one hundred wines are sold by the bottle. Closed at weekends.

KEMIA BAR AT MOMO

25 Heddon Street, W1
Tel: 0171 434 4040
It is almost impossible to get into this trendy bar situated in the basement of the popular Moroccan restaurant. The drinks and bar snacks, however, are fantastic and it is well worth the effort.

HANOVER SQUARE

25 Hanover Square, W1
Tel: 0171 408 0935
Situated close to Oxford Circus, this basement wine bar is a popular meeting place after work and serves good food with a choice of over two hundred different wines, many by the glass.

MASH

19–21 Great Portland Street, W1
Tel: 0171 637 5555
The bar takes up most of the ground floor with a restaurant on the first floor. At the back is the brewery of gleaming stainless steel, protected behind glass, while the chrome bar runs down one side. A wide variety of drinks and lots to watch.

METROPOLITAN BAR

Old Park Lane, W1
Tel: 0171 447 1000
To get in after five o'clock in the afternoon you need to be on the two-thousand-only membership list or a resident at the hotel. The bar has a large standing area and curvaceous red-leather banquettes, with cocktails of mouth-watering combinations.

SHAMPERS

4 Kingly Street, W1
Tel: 0171 437 1692
Good selection of wines and reasonable bistro-style food maintain the popularity of this Soho-based wine bar.

PUBS

THE GUINEA

30 Bruton Place, W1
Tel: 0171 499 1210
The reputation of this pub is due more to its food than anything else. It is famous for its steak and steak-and-kidney pies, consumed in the old-fashioned atmosphere of its upstairs dining room.

NEWMAN ARMS

23 Rathbone Street, W1
Tel: 0171 636 1127
This pub is famous for its much-coveted home-made pies, which are covered in thick pastry. Lunch is served upstairs in a small wooden room with deep red-velvet seats.

RED LION

23 Crown Passage off Pall Mall, SW1
Te: 0171 930 4141
Tucked away down a tiny cobbled alleyway off Pall Mall, the Red Lion is reputed to be one of the oldest pubs in the West End. A restaurant on the first floor serves traditional British food.

RED LION

2 Duke of York Street, SW1
Tel: 0171 930 2030
Notable for its beautiful oak-panelled bar with a mirrored back, a central bar splits the pub into two narrow rooms. A small pub, it is popular with the smart slightly older set, inclined to do their shopping in the area.

RUNNING FOOTMAN

5 Charles Street, W1
Tel: 0171 499 2988
A cosy pub just off Berkeley Square with comfortable seating and a roaring fire in winter. In the eighteenth century a "running footman" was a common sight, clearing any obstacles in the path of his master's coach.

YE GRAPES

16 Shepherd Market, W1
Tel: 0171 499 1563
A pub full of character, its walls and bar covered by glass cases of stuffed fish and game, interspersed with paintings, mirrors and antique whisky kegs.

DELICATESSENS, COFFEE AND JUICE BARS

AMATO

14 Old Compton St, W1
Tel: 0171 734 5733
A relative newcomer, the former chef from Patisserie Valerie has opened up his own cafe serving delicious homemade pastries and cakes.

AURORA

49 Lexington Street, W1
Tel: 0171 494 0514
A relaxing and homely spot with a nice courtyard, this Soho cafe serves good coffee and cakes in addition to other more healthy dishes.

BAR ITALIA

22 Frith Street, W1
Tel: 0171 437 4520

Classic twenty-four hour Soho coffee shop, which has been trading for over forty years and is still considered to be the best place after a night on the town.

CAFFE NERO

225 Regent Street, W1
Tel: 0171 491 8899
High round tables and counters topped with marble, matched by chrome chairs with black wicker seats provide a perfect setting for delectable coffee and cakes.

EMPORIUM COFFEE BAR

42 James Street, W1
Tel: 0171 224 1493
Home-made cakes and fresh coffee combined with a relaxed and friendly atmosphere, and a light Continental menu make this a popular spot.

FORTNUM AND MASON

181 Piccadilly, W1
Tel: 0171 734 8040
There are three restaurants to try in this world-famous store, whether it is coffee or a traditional English tea, or a proper lunch you are after. Service is unhurried and professional.

LA MADELEINE

5 Vigo Street, W1
Te. 0171 734 8353
Just off Regent Street and Savile Row this cafe is so French you would be forgiven for thinking you were in Paris. In addition to coffee and patiseries, snacks and larger meals are available.

MAISON BERTAUX

28 Greek Street, W1
Tel: 0171 437 6007
London's oldest patisserie was established in Soho in 1871, and still enjoys a loyal following.

MILDREDS

58 Greek Street, W1
Tel: 0171 494 1634

Vegetarian food is the speciality and the imaginative meals are delicious, ensuring that this Soho cafe is always full to capacity.

PATISSERIE VALERIE

44 Old Compton Street, W1
Tel: 0171 437 3466
The original location for this world-famous chain of coffee houses, which now has branches all over London.

RANDALL & AUBIN

16 Brewer Street, W1
Tel: 0171 287 4447
Simple rotisserie fare and seafood is eaten at the counter of this Soho deli/diner.

MALE ELEGANCE

BATES

21a Jermyn Street, SW1
Tel: 0171 734 2722
With a shop window full of hats of all different shapes and sizes, Bates has a worldwide reputation for some of the best Panama hats.

BERRY BROS. & RUDD LTD.

3 St James's Street, SW1
Tel: 0171 396 9600
Thee hundred years of tradition are reflected in the venerable premises of this established wine merchant.

BUDD

1A & 3 Piccadilly Arcade, W1
Tel: 0171 493 0139
Bespoke shirtmaker has a wide range of ready-to-wear accessories for white- and black-tie occasions. Custom-made formal shirts have not changed since 1910.

GEO F. TRUMPER

9 Curzon Street, W1
Tel: 0171 499 1850
Well-known barbers whose shop is filled with after-shave lotions, shaving brushes with special bristles and other gentlemen's luxuries.

BESPOKE TAILORS

Douglas Hayward
95 Mount Street, W1
Tel: 0171 499 5574

Gieves & Hawkes Ltd.
1 Savile Row, W1
Tel: 0171 434 2001

John Pearse
6 Mead Street, W1
Tel: 0171 434 0738

Mark Powell & Co.
17 Newburgh Street, W1
Tel: 0171 287 5498

Richard James
31 Savile Row, W1
Tel: 0171 434 0605
(see page 157)

HERBERT JOHNSON
54 St James's Street, SW1
Tel: 0171 408 1174
Less venerable than Lock's but no less important as a hatter to the discerning public.

HOLLAND & HOLLAND LTD.
31 Bruton Street, W1
Tel: 0171 499 4411
Another bastion of the hunting, shooting and fishing set.

JAMES LOCK & CO. LTD.
6 St James's Street, SW1
Tel: 0171 930 5849
Bespoke hatters for over 300 years, Lock's provide a wide range of headwear for all occasions to the discerning gentleman and lady.

JAMES PURDEY & SONS LTD.
Audley House
57 South Audley Street, W1
Tel: 0171 499 1801
Accepted as one of the greatest names in gunmaking, Purdey's premises in the heart of Mayfair have the atmosphere of a gentlemen's club, with racks of guns, each with individual and beautifully engraved butts, enclosed in antique glass-fronted cabinets.

JOHN LOBB
9 St James's Street, SW1
0171 930 3664
Skilled bespoke bootmakers select and match lengths of leather for a pair of hand-crafted shoes, as they have done over the centuries. Individual moulds, of the feet of their clients from around the world, are stored in great racks in the basement of the shop.

LONGMIRE
12 Bury Street, W1
Tel: 0171 930 8720
A shop which specialises in cuff-links with more than one thousand pairs whether new, ready-to-wear or custom-made.

MILROYS OF SOHO LTD.
3 Greek Street, W1
Tel: 0171 437 0893
A shop in Soho which specialises in whisky and offers a fantastic choice and expertise.

NEW & LINGWOOD
53 Jermyn Street, SW1
Tel: 0171 493 9621
Like Turnbull & Asser, highly regarded as shirtmakers.

SWAINE ADENEY BRIGG
54 St James's Street, SW1
Tel: 0171 409 7277
Gentlemen's accessories, such as walking sticks and umbrellas.

TURNBULL & ASSER
71 & 72 Jermyn Street, SW1
Tel: 0171 930 0502
World-wide reputation as bespoke shirtmakers.

ANTIQUE SHOPS AND AUCTION HOUSES

ALISTAIR SAMPSON
120 Mount Street, W1
Tel: 0171 409 1799
Early and fine English furniture, pottery, pictures and oriental works of art.

ANTOINE CHENEVIERE FINE ARTS
27 Bruton Street, W1
Tel: 0171 491 1007
Eighteenth- and nineteenth-century furniture and paintings from Russia, Italy, Austria, Sweden and Germany.

CHRISTIE'S
8 King Street, SW1
Tel: 0171 839 9060

COLEFAX & FOWLER
39 Brook Street, W1
Tel: 0171 493 2231
Best known for its fabrics and interior design, the London showroom has a selection of eighteenth- and nineteenth-century French and English furniture on display in Nancy Lancaster's former drawing room, sold under the Sybil Colefax & John Fowler arm of the business.

MALLETT & SON
141 New Bond Street, W1
Tel: 0171 499 7411
Top quality eighteenth-century English furniture and works of art.

MALLETT AT BOURDON HOUSE
2 Davies Street, W1
Tel: 0171 629 2444
Decorative and continental furniture and works of art.

PHILLIPS
New Bond Street, W1
Tel: 0171 629 6602

SOTHEBY'S
34–35 New Bond Street, W1
Tel: 0171 493 8080

STAIR & COMPANY
14 Mount Street, W1
Tel: 0171 499 1784
eighteenth century English furniture, mirrors, chandeliers and works of art.

MUSEUMS

APSLEY HOUSE
149 Piccadilly, W1
Tel: 0171 499 5676
Former home of the Duke of Wellington, Apsley House has undergone a major refurbishment over the last few years.

ROYAL ACADEMY OF ARTS
Burlington House
Piccadilly, W1
Tel: 0171 300 8000
Famous for its annual Summer Exhibition and temporary exhibitions of art.

SPENCER HOUSE
St James's Place, SW1
Tel: 0171 499 8620
Open to the public on Sundays only, this beautiful building was the former London home of the Spencer family.

THE WALLACE COLLECTION
Hertford House
Manchester Square, W1
Tel: 0171 935 0687
This private collection of French eighteenth-century paintings, porcelain and furniture was bequeathed to the nation by the widow of Sir Richard Wallace in 1897 (see page 172, 173, 181).

Covent Garden, Holborn and the Strand

HOTELS

COVENT GARDEN HOTEL
10 Monmouth Street, WC2
Tel: 0171 806 1000
A five-star hotel at the centre of Covent Garden, this is a good place to stay for a weekend dedicated to culture.

THE HOWARD
Temple Place, WC2
Tel: 0171 836 3555
Preferred by businessmen for its location quietly removed from the bustle of Covent Garden with magnificent views over the river.

LE MERIDIEN WALDORF
Aldwych, WC2
Tel: 0171 836 2400
In the heart of theatreland and located on the edge of Covent Garden, this hotel finds itself centre stage.

ONE ALDWYCH
WC2
Tel: 0171 300 1000
Only recently open, this hot new hotel at the end of the Strand is already proving to be very popular with the smart set in London.

THE SAVOY
Strand, WC2
Tel: 0171 836 4343
Bastion of good service and good taste, the reputation of The Savoy as a sophisticated hotel has spread throughout the world.

RESTAURANTS

BANK
1 Kingsway, WC2
Tel: 0171 379 9797
A new brasserie with colourful modern British cooking at Aldwych, serving an excellent breakfast. A good place to meet before the theatre.

BOULEVARD
40 Wellington Street, WC2
Tel: 0171 240 2992
Good French farmhouse-style food and fast service make this Covent Garden brasserie an ideal pre-theatre restaurant.

CAFE PACIFICO
5 Langley Street, WC2
Tel: 0171 379 7728
The best Mexican food in a noisy atmosphere continues the popularity of this Covent Garden cantina.

FOOD FOR THOUGHT
31 Neal Street, WC2
Tel: 0171 836 0239
Despite the queue, the tasty vegetarian food is well worth the wait in this basement restaurant in the heart of Covent Garden.

FRYER'S DELIGHT
19 Theobald's Road, WC1
Tel: 0171 405 4114
The local fish and chip restaurant just off Gray's Inn offers the best fish and value for money.

INDIA CLUB
143 Strand, WC2
Tel: 0171 836 0650
This Aldwych institution serves great food and delicious curries and is very popular. It is unlicensed so you must bring your own (BYO).

THE IVY
1 West Street, WC2
Tel: 0171 836 4751
Regarded as one of the best restaurants in London, with charming service and a delicious British menu, its clubby panelled interior is a favourite with theatre-goers and stars alike.

JOE ALLEN
13 Exeter Street, WC2
Tel: 0171 836 0651
American food and particularly the "off-menu" burgers add to the exciting atmosphere of this underground restaurant in Covent Garden.

MANZI'S
1 Leicester Street, WC2
Tel: 0171 734 0224
A good, old-fashioned fish parlour in the heart of London's theatreland with reliable and well-cooked food.

MON PLAISIR
21 Monmouth Street, WC2
Tel: 0171 836 7243
Very good French food with lunches and pre-theatre menus at special prices.

MUSEUM STREET CAFE
47 Museum Street, WC2
Tel: 0171 405 3211
Good modern British food and service to match in this minimal cafe near the British Museum.

NEAL STREET
26 Neal Street, WC2
Tel: 0171 836 8368
Well-known Italian restaurant owned by the man famous for mushrooms, Antonio Carluccio.

LE PALAIS DU JARDIN
136 Long Acre, WC2
Tel: 0171 379 5353
This huge Covent Garden brasserie is always packed, the atmosphere is cheerful and its food is good value for money. Particular favourites are the seafood platters.

POONS
4 Leicester Street, WC2
Tel: 0171 437 1528
A Chinese restaurant located in the centre of theatreland with a reliable menu.

RULES
35 Maiden Lane, WC2
Tel: 836 5314
London's oldest restaurant, Rules has been open since 1798 and, despite its attraction to tourists, still manages to retain much of its authentic period charm. Good British food and wonderful puddings.

SAVOY GRILL
Strand, WC2
Tel: 0171 836 4343
The classic dining room at The Savoy, favoured by businessmen and politicians alike, has the best service.

SAVOY RIVER RESTAURANT
Strand, WC2
Tel: 0171 420 2699
Anglo-French cuisine and a spectacular setting–particularly if seated by the window with views over the Thames. A great place for an unhurried, luxury breakfast.

SIMPSONS-IN-THE-STRAND
100 Strand, WC2
Tel: 0171 836 9112
The definitive English breakfast is still to be found in the old-fashioned dining hall of this Edwardian restaurant, although lunch and dinner tend to cater more for the tourist.

BARS

AMERICAN BAR
The Savoy
Strand, WC2
Tel: 0171 836 4343
A London institution for the past sixty years, its reputation is undiminished. One of the few bars where a dress code is still important, the cocktails are some of the best in the city.

BRASSERIE MAX AT COVENT GARDEN HOTEL
10 Monmouth Street, WC2
Tel: 0171 806 1000
An understated bar at this five-star hotel is frequented by a fashionable crowd, who come for the relaxed atmosphere. There is an international brasserie menu at lunchtime.

CORK & BOTTLE
44–46 Cranbourn Street, WC2
Tel: 0171 734 7807
A cosy cellar next to a sex shop in Leicester Square has a lively and fun atmosphere with a good selection of wine.

PUBS

MUSEUM TAVERN
Museum Street, WC2
Tel: 0171 242 8987
There has been a pub on this site for several hundred years and the present building dates from the 1760s when the British Museum opened across the street.

DELICATESSENS, COFFEE AND JUICE BARS

THE BRITISH MUSEUM CAFE RESTAURANT
The British Museum
Bloomsbury, WC1
Tel: 0171 636 1555
It is reassuring to know that there is somewhere to collapse over a coffee and a light meal after a serious cultural morning. This cafe at the entrance to the British Museum has everything one could possibly want.

GARDEN CAFE
32 Museum Street, WC1
Tel: 0171 637 4309
American/Continental
patisserie near the
British Museum serves
a good breakfast and
light lunch.

JUICE
7 Earlham Street, WC2
Tel: 0171 836 7376
In an ambience of bare white
walls and coloured glass
tables, juices are squeezed
to order and the milk
shakes are thick and healthy.
Sandwiches and delicious
coffee.

**MONMOUTH COFFEE
HOUSE**
27 Monmouth Street,
WC2
Tel: 0171 836 5272
Established twenty years ago
and located opposite the
main Neal's Yard complex

of shops and boutiques, the
Monmouth Coffee House
specialises in importing and
roasting a wide variety of coffee. A sampling room at the
back of the shop gives
customers an opportunity to
taste before they buy.

**NEAL'S YARD
BEACH CAFE**
13 Neal's Yard,
WC2
Tel: 0171 240 1168
Bright and friendly with free
newspapers, good coffee and
a range of juices squeezed
to order.

NEAL'S YARD DAIRY
WC2
Renowned for its speciality
shops, the selection at Neal's
Yard ranges from cheese,
bread and patisseries, to boutiques focusing on aro-
matherapy and health
remedies.

THE WALDORF MERIDIEN
Aldwych, WC2
Tel: 0171 836 2400
Today this hotel is one of the
last bastions of the famous
tea-dance which is held in
the Palm Court. With obvious appeal to tourists, The
Waldorf is also gaining
a reputation for its buffet
breakfasts.

MUSEUMS

THE BRITISH MUSEUM
Great Russell Street, WC1
Tel: 0171 636 1555
One could spend days in the
British Museum, there is so
much to see. A wonderful
surprise was finding the
empty hall which once
housed the books, now
found at the new British
Library, on Euston Road,
NW1. After restoration, this
will be the new home for the
Museum of Mankind, which

is moving back from
Burlington Gardens.

**THE COURTAULD
INSTITUTE GALLERY**
Somerset House
Strand,
WC2
Tel: 0171 873 2526
A very fine collection of
Old Masters, as well as
Impressionist and Post-
Impressionist art on
display in 11 galleries.
Temporary exhibitions
highlight the gallery's
fascinating collection.

**DICKENS' HOUSE
MUSEUM**
48 Doughty Street,
WC1
Tel: 0171 405 2127
Situated just off the Gray's
Inn Road, this Georgian
townhouse was one of
author Charles Dickens's
former homes.

NATIONAL GALLERY
Trafalgar Square, WC2
Tel: 0171 839 3321
One of the world's finest
permanent collections of
Western European paintings.

**NATIONAL PORTRAIT
GALLERY**
St Martin's Place, WC2
Tel: 0171 306 0055
Permanent collection of
portraits of the famous
and infamous.

**SIR JOHN SOANE'S
MUSEUM**
13 Lincoln's Inn Fields, WC2
Tel: 0171 405 2107
This townhouse on the outskirts of the City was bought
by Sir Soane to house his collection of classical busts, statues, and treasures which
accumulated over the years.
Maintained as it would have
been during his lifetime, it is
a unique museum.

Hampstead

HOTELS

LANGORF
20 Frognal, NW3
Tel: 0171 794 0101
A comfortable townhouse,
ideally located in the centre
of Hampstead.

**THE LONDON BED &
BREAKFAST AGENCY**
71 Fellows Road, NW3
Tel: 0171 586 2768
This agency holds a list of
selected private homes which
provide the opportunity to
get to know the real London.
Homes in the centre of
London cost around £30
per person per night and
become less expensive as you
move further out.

SWISS COTTAGE
4 Adamson Road, NW3

Tel: 0171 722 2281
A Victorian townhouse tradi-
tionally decorated with
antique furniture. Fifty-eight
rooms, no restaurant.

RESTAURANTS

BYRON'S
3a Downshire Hill, NW3
Tel: 0171 435 3544
Modern British cuisine
is the order of the day
at this Hampstead town-
house located in a quiet
side street.

LA CAGE IMAGINAIRE
16 Flask Walk, NW3
Tel: 0171 794 6674
Located in a Hampstead
backwater, this French
restaurant offers set menus
for both lunch and dinner
which are good value.

CUCINA
45a South End Road, NW3
Tel: 0171 435 7814
This trendy restaurant serves
fresh innovative British
cuisine and is considered to
be one of the best in
Hampstead.

GUNG-HO
330–332 West End Lane,
NW6
Tel: 0171 794 1444
This Chinese restaurant in
West Hampstead provides a
wide range of unusual dishes
in an attractive modern
surrounding.

**HOUSE ON ROSSLYN
HILL**
34a Rosslyn Hill, NW3
Tel: 0171 435 8037
Part of the young Hampstead
scene, this is the place to

read the Sunday newspapers
and rub shoulders with the
locals.

NAUTILUS
27 Fortune Green Road,
NW6
Tel: 0171 435 2532
A good and reliable West
Hampstead fish and chip
restaurant.

ZEN
83 Hampstead High Street,
NW3
Tel: 0171 794 7863
Clean and flavoursome Chinese cuisine is served in a
sparse modern decor.

BARS

BAR ROOM BAR
48 Rosslyn Hill, NW3
Tel: 0171 435 0808

A cool white cube of a room
with a glass and wood bar
right in the middle. Wooden
seat coverings with Latin
inscriptions and a tented
conservatory behind the
main bar make this bar a
mecca for Hampstead
sophisticates.

PUBS

THE FLASK
14 Flask Walk, NW3
Tel: 0171 435 4580
Charming Victorian pub
just off Hampstead High
Street which serves above
average food.

FREEMASONS ARMS
32 Downshire Hill, NW3
Tel: 0171 433 6811
Dating from 1819, this pub
has the largest and best beer

garden in Hampstead. Food is good and there is also a respectable wine list.

KING WILLIAM IV
75 Hampstead High Street, NW3
Tel: 0171 435 5747
Opposite some of Hampstead's most expensive clothes shops, this pub—attracting a loyal gay following and their friends—has a beautiful panelled interior with large bow windows. Sunday lunch can be bought for £5 and there is also a very good crêperie next to the small outdoor beer garden.

SPANIARD'S INN
Spaniard's Lane, NW3
Tel: 0181 731 6571

Once the favourite watering hole of the famous highwayman Dick Turpin, this historic pub has creaky stairs and oak-panelled rooms. Its long bar is the resting place of many a walker on the Heath.

YE OLDE WHITE BEAR
New End, NW3
Tel: 0171 435 3758
Located not far from the Heath, this pub is furnished with a motley collection of old chairs, sofas and church pews. Good food and house wine.

CAFES

BREWHOUSE CAFE
Kenwood House
Hampstead Lane, NW6
Tel: 0181 341 5384
The Brewhouse was formerly a domestic wing to Kenwood House, which sits in a beautiful park surrounded by trees, adjoining Hampstead Heath.
The lawns run down to a lake, where open-air concerts are held on summer evenings. The cafe has a lunch menu and also serves afternoon tea.

CAFE BIANCO
12 Perrins Court, NW3
Just off Hampstead High Street, this charming cafe offers a varied menu which changes daily and also delivers locally without charge.
Good place for sitting outside.

MUSEUMS

FENTON HOUSE
20 Hampstead Grove, NW3
Tel: 0171 435 3471
This William & Mary house, which was built in 1693, is the oldest manor house in Hampstead. Now maintained by the National Trust, it houses two exhibitions which are open to the public during the summer–the Benton-Fletcher collection of early keyboard instruments and a collection of porcelain put together by Lady Binning, the last owner of Fenton.

FREUD MUSEUM
20 Maresfield Garden, NW3
Tel: 0171 435 2002
Home of Sigmund Freud for the last two years of his life (see page 179).

KEATS HOUSE
Keats Grove, NW3
Tel: 0171435 2062
Home to the poet John Keats from 1818, his house was first opened to the public in 1925.

KENWOOD HOUSE
Hampstead Lane, NW3
Tel: 0181 348 1286
Situated just inside Hampstead Heath, where it was first built in 1616, Kenwood was transformed by Robert Adam in 1764 and has a wonderful library. The grounds extend down towards a lake where summer concerts are performed in the open air.

Islington

RESTAURANTS

CASALE FRANCO
134–137 Upper Street, N1
Tel: 0171 226 8994
Good Italian food and excellent pizzas continue to draw in the crowds at this Islington favourite, located down a small alley.

GRANITA
127 Upper Street, N1
Tel: 0171 226 3222
Modern British cooking is served at this imaginative restaurant, popular with Islington locals. Small with wooden chairs and tables.

KAVANAGH'S
26 Penton Street, N1
Tel: 0171 833 1380
Good modern British cooking and charming service ensure the popularity of this cheap and small Islington restaurant.

LOLA'S
359 Upper Street, N1
Tel: 0171 359 1932
In the heart of the antique centre of Islington, Lola's features an eclectic menu.

PASHA
301 Upper Street, N1
Tel: 0171 226 1454
A friendly Turkish restaurant with very good set menus.

LA PIRAGUA
176 Upper Street, N1
Tel: 0171 354 2843
Cheap, cheerful and very full plates of delicious Columbian food make this restaurant popular for customers on a budget.

UPPER STREET FISH SHOP
324 Upper Street, N1
Tel: 0171 359 1401
Wonderful fresh fish and seafood and surprisingly low prices combined with a friendly atmosphere. Bring your own drinks.

THE WHITE ONION
297 Upper Street, N1
Tel: 0171 359 3533
Another modern British restaurant in this Islington street, the White Onion is a relative newcomer and doing well.

BARS

BARTIZAN
3–5 Islington High Street, N1
Tel: 0171 833 9595
A large and comfortable interior, where food is prepared under the public gaze through an opening to the right of the long bar. Good cocktails.

PUBS

ALBION
10 Thornhill Road, N1
Tel: 0171 607 7450
A cosy pub, its patio gardens lined with trees, attracts a mixed crowd of locals from Barnsbury.

ALMEIDA THEATRE BAR
1 Almeida Street, N1
Tel: 0171 226 0931
This bar at London's trendiest small theatre is not limited to theatre-goers but is open to the general public. Noted for its long bar, the food is good—if expensive—and the walls are covered with stylish photographs.

KINGS HEAD
115 Upper Street, N1
Tel: 0171 226 1916
Probably the oldest pub theatre in London, where plays and musicals are often staged. Full of atmosphere, serving good beer, the staff are known to quote your bill in pounds, shillings and pence.

DELICATESSENS, COFFEE AND JUICE BARS

ANGEL CAFE BAR
65 Graham Street, N1
Tel: 0171 608 2656
Simple and fresh decoration with chrome tables or comfortable sofas to choose from. Newspapers are provided with a wonderfully imaginative vegetarian menu.

CAFE PASTA
8 Theberton Street, N1
Tel: 0171 704 9089
Located between The Almeida and The King's Head—Islington's two theatres—and close to Camden Passage Antiques Market, this cafe is charming and stylish. Downstairs is bright and modern, while the first floor is decorated in the style of an Edwardian dining room.

THE RHYTHMIC
89–91 Chapel Market, N1
Tel: 0171 713 5859
Britain's biggest jazz venue,
The Rhythmic plays host to
many music legends and puts
on shows at night. During
the daytime, it divides into
two, with the jazz club at the
back and, at the front, a
welcoming cafe bar made
out of beaten metal. Wide
variety of coffee and delicious lunch snacks on offer.

ANTIQUE SHOPS AND DEALERS

CAMDEN PASSAGE
The Angel
Islington, N1
Over 200 shops and 150 stalls
line this paved pedestrian
precinct selling antiques, furniture and collectibles. Most

of the shops are open Tues-
day–Saturday. Market days
are Wednesday and Saturday,
while on Thursday mornings
there are second-hand and
antiquarian book stalls.

ECCENTRICITIES
94–98 Islington High Street,
N1
Tel: 0171 359 9894
Recently opened on the site
of Keith Skeel's former
antique shop, Eccentricities
is another of his ventures,
specialising in fun and reasonably cheap decorative
objects and furniture.

HERITAGE ANTIQUES
112 Islington High Street
Camden Passage, N1
Tel: 0171 226 7789
Oak and country furniture,
seventeenth–nineteenth

century European metalwork
and decorative objects.

KEITH SKEEL ANTIQUES
46 Essex Road, N1
Tel: 0171 359 5633
Specialises in English
and Continental furniture
and decorative items
(see pages 93 and 94).

LINDA GUMB
9 Camden Passage, N1
Tel: 0171 354 1184
Seventeenth–nineteenth
century tapestries, cushions
and objects.

TWENTIETH CENTURY DESIGN
274 Upper Street, N1
Tel: 0171 288 1996
Furniture and lighting from
1935 to the present day with
classics by Charles Eames,

Alvar Aalto, George Nelson
and others.

SHOPS

FRANK GODFREY LTD.
7 Highbury Park, N5
Tel: 0171 226 2425
Organic butcher who
delivers throughout London
and also sells cheese,
chutneys and other
organic foods.

LA FROMAGERIE
Highbury Park, N5
Tel: 0171 359 7440
Simply delicious cheese.

MUSEUMS

CRAFT COUNCIL
44a Pentonville Road,
N1
Tel: 0171 278 7700

Exhibitions of contemporary
crafts, pottery, textiles and
jewellery with possibilities for
commissions.

THE ESTORICK COLLECTION OF MODERN ITALIAN ART
Northampton Lodge
39a Canonbury Square,
N1
Tel: 0171 704 9522
This is a relatively new
museum of modern Italian
art which is based on the
collection created by Eric
Estorick (1913–93) who was
an American sociologist,
collector and dealer.
His collection is housed
in Northampton Lodge,
a smart late-Georgian
building which was
restored by the architect
Nathanial Gee.

Clerkenwell, Smithfield and Spitalfields

HOTELS

GREAT EASTERN HOTEL
Liverpool Street, EC
Redevelopment is underway
of the only hotel in the City
of London. An ambitious
project to be tackled by Conran Holdings and Arcadian
International, the Great Eastern is due to open on the
cusp of the new century in
Autumn 1999 with 265 bed-
rooms and seven restaurants
and bars.

RESTAURANTS

1 LOMBARD STREET
1 Lombard Street, EC3
Tel.: 0171 929 6611
Another French restaurant
recently with a successful
combination of top chef,
Herbert Berger, and a glam-
ourous location—the listed
banking hall of the Scottish

Provident building—which
houses the main brasserie,
with a smaller restaurant at
the back.

CAFÉ DU MARCHE
22 Charterhouse Square,
EC1
Tel: 0171 608 1609
A French "country" restaurant on the fringe of Smithfield market.

THE CLERKENWELL
73 Clerkenwell Road, EC1
Tel: 0171 831 7595
Good and flavoursome
Italian cooking.

NOVELLI
30 Clerkenwell Green, EC1
Tel: 0171 251 6606
Delicious as well as good
value for money, the
brasserie section of Maison
Novelli has moved recently
to its own building.

THE QUALITY CHOP HOUSE
94 Farringdon Road, EC1
Tel: 0171 837 5093
This restored working class
caterer in Clerkenwell serves
good British fare in a
functional rather stark
atmosphere.

BARS

BETJEMANS
43–44 Cloth Fair, EC1
Tel: 0171 600 7778
Unpretentious wine bar with
a good selection of wines
and champagnes looks out
over St Bartholomew's
church and some of the
oldest streets of London.

BLEEDING HEART
Bleeding Heart Yard
off Greville Street, EC1
Tel: 0171 242 2056
Located just off Hatton Gar-

den, the jewellery centre of
London, Bleeding Heart
remains one of the city's
more interesting wine bars.
Downstairs is now a restaurant with white tablecloths
and French waiters, while the
wine bar on the ground floor
remains little changed.

THE FENCE
67–69 Cowcross Street, EC1
Tel: 0171 250 3414
The very good wine list
always offers something new
and there is a garden in
which to enjoy it.

MATCH
45–47 Clerkenwell Rd, EC1
Tel: 0171 250 4002
Atlantic blue walls and
frosted glass panels, steel pil-
lars and subdued lighting
with a sunken bar on the
ground floor. Cocktails
and a vast assortment of

Martini and champagne
specials.

PUBS

BLACK FRIAR
174 Queen Victoria St, EC4
Tel: 0171 236 5650
An unlikely interior and an
extraordinary wedge-shaped
exterior, this pub perches on
the edge of the City on the
site of the medieval Blackfriars Monastery (see p. 192).

THE EAGLE
159 Farringdon Road, EC1
Tel: 0171 837 1353
Busy and very noisy City
fringe pub with a good
reputation for its
Mediterranean-style food.

FOX & ANCHOR
115 Charterhouse Street,
EC1
Tel: 0171 253 4838

Good beer, wonderful mixed grills and the advantage of a license which runs from 7:00 a.m. make this pub one of the best places in London for breakfast.

HAND & SHEARS
1 Middle Street, EC1
Tel: 0171 253 4838
Built in the sixteenth century, this small traditional pub with a wood-panelled bar, is one of the oldest in the City.

HOPE & SIR LOIN
94 Cowcross Street, EC1
Tel: 0171 253 8525
Delicious breakfast and the best fillet steak in town maintain the popularity of this Smithfield pub.

DELICATESSENS, COFFEE AND JUICE BARS

AL'S
11–13 Exmouth Market, EC1
Tel: 0171 837 4821
A relaxed all-day cafe in Clerkenwell, where an endless breakfast is served amongst other tasty things.

ARKANSAS CAFE
Old Spitalfield Market, E1
Tel: 0171 377 6999
This very simple cafe has the reputation for the best BBQ steak, burgers and ribs in London.

ASHBY'S
4 Artillery Passage, E1
Tel: 0171 247 1830
A few minutes walk from Spitalfields Market and located down a narrow alleyway, this intimate coffee house is concealed behind a Regency façade. A good selection of sandwiches and coffee can be consumed on the premises or taken away.

BRICK LANE BEIGEL BAKE
159 Brick Lane, E1
Tel: 0171 729 0616
Fresh bagels, apple tarts and cheesecake, salt-beef sandwiches and other delicacies can be found at this great East End cafe.

MALE ELEGANCE

J. AMESBURY & CO.
32 Elder Street, E1
Tel: 0171 377 2006
Jason Amesbury trained with John Lobb, London's

most famous bootmaker, and set up on his own in 1995 as a bespoke shoe-maker in the basement of Timothy Everest's townhouse in Spitalfields.

TIMOTHY EVEREST LTD.
32 Elder Street, E1
Tel: 0171 377 5770
A bespoke tailor who moved his business from the West End and set up shop in a Georgian terraced house in the heart of Spitalfields, Timothy Everest has gained a world-wide reputation in the design of men's clothes (see pages 157–158).

MUSEUMS

THE BARBICAN
Barbican Centre, EC2
Tel: 0171 588 9023
Many attractions are available under the one roof, including concerts, exhibitions and several restaurants. The Barbican is also home to the Royal Shakespeare Company.

DENNIS SEVERS
18 Folgate Street, E1
Tel: 0171 247 4013
Dennis opens his unique

Georgian home on the first Sunday and Monday evenings of each month. A unique opportunity to witness how life in Georgian London must have been. Booking essential.

DR. JOHNSON'S HOUSE
17 Gough Square, EC4
Tel: 0171 353 3745
Located off a cobbled court-yard behind Fleet Street, No. 17 was one of many houses which Dr. Samuel Johnson rented during his lifetime. He goes down in history as the man who compiled the first comprehensive English dictionary in 1755 (see page 179).

GEFFRYE MUSEUM
Kingsland Road, E2
Tel: 0171 739 9893
Located in Hackney, the Geffrye Museum was originally the site of fourteen alms houses which were built in 1715. Its permanent displays of fully furnished rooms date from the Elizabethan age to the 1930s and provide a unique insight into the historical development of house interiors.

MUSEUM OF LONDON
150 London Wall, EC2
0171 600 3699
The museum has a new eighteenth-century gallery which illustrates life as it would have been in the well-off houses of Georgian London, to the accompaniment of music of the period.

WHITECHAPEL GALLERY
Whitechapel High Street, E1
Tel: 0171 522 7888
This gallery has gained a deserved reputation as an innovator in the art world.

WILLIAM MORRIS GALLERY
Lloyd Park
Forest Road, E17
Tel: 0171 527 3782
Built in 1750, this is the childhood home of William Morris, designer, craftsman, poet and socialist, whose name is associated with the Edwardian movement in interior design and decoration. It contains major examples of his textiles, wallpaper and furniture, as well as work by the Arts & Craft movement which he inspired.

Docklands and the Southbank

RESTAURANTS

THE APPRENTICE
31 Shad Thames, SE1
Tel: 0171 234 0254
Good modern British cooking, combined with an unusual style of service and super value, make this chefs' school beside Tower Bridge, an interesting choice.

BENGAL CLIPPER
Shad Thames, SE1
Tel: 0171 357 9001

A large and comfortable Indian restaurant serves authentic and unusual dishes.

BISTROT 2 RIVERSIDE
Oxo Tower Wharf, SE1
Tel: 0171 401 8200
A brasserie located on the second floor of the Oxo Tower—with a less spectacular view than its loftier restaurant upstairs—is bright and welcoming with an eclectic menu.

BLUE PRINT CAFE
Design Museum
Butler's Wharf, SE1
Tel: 0171 378 7031
An interesting menu in this modern cafe, where there is a conservatory with spectacular views of Tower Bridge.

THE BUTLER'S WHARF CHOP-HOUSE
36e Shad Thames, SE1
Tel: 0171 403 3403
Good English food is served

at this riverside restaurant overlooking Tower Bridge, one of the Conran-inspired locations this side of the river. Brunch is recommended.

FINA ESTAMPA
150 Tooley Street, SE1
Tel: 0171 403 1342
A husband and wife team serve wonderful Peruvian home cooking from premises close to Tower Bridge.

LIVEBAIT
43 The Cut, SE1
Tel: 0171 928 7211
Wonderful imaginative seafood makes this the best place for fish in London. Located near Waterloo station.

MEZZANINE
National Theatre
South Bank, SE1
Tel: 0171 928 3531
An in-house restaurant serving modern British

cuisine at the National Theatre.

LE PONT DE LA TOUR
36d Shad Thames, SE1
Tel: 0171 403 8403
Good modern French cooking and a spectacular view of the river in sophisticated surroundings continue to make this a popular lunch and dinner restaurant. The separate Bar & Grill serves delicious shellfish and other snacks.

BARS

ARCHDUKE WINE BAR
Arch 153
Concert Hall Approach, SE1
Tel: 0171 928 9370
A large wine bar/restaurant, with a good value wine list, situated under a railway arch near the South Bank Centre, makes this a good meeting place.

MESON DON FELIPE
53 The Cut, SE1
Tel: 0171 928 3237
A crowded tiny bar near the Old Vic theatre offers good tapas and wine.

THE WATERLOO FIRE STATION
150 Waterloo Road, SE1
Tel: 0171 401 3267

Reasonably priced British food is available at this large bar/refectory near the Old Vic theatre.

PUBS

MAYFLOWER
117 Rotherhithe Street, SE16
Tel: 0171 237 4088
A busy riverside inn built on the site of a sixteenth-century tavern called the Shippe. It was renamed after the vessel that took the pilgrims to America.

GEORGE INN
77 Borough High Street, SE1
Tel: 0171 407 2056
London's only surviving galleried coaching inn, the George is another pub steeped in history. It holds a small beer festival every month.

MARKET PORTER
9 Stoney Street, SE1
Tel: 0171 407 2495
Oak beams and time-worn furniture with several real ales on tap with the advantage of being open early in the morning to cater for the market traders at the nearby Borough Market.

DELICATESSENS, COFFEE AND JUICE BARS

KONDITOR AND COOK AT THE YOUNG VIC THEATRE
66 The Cut, SE1
Tel: 0171 620 2700
A stylish cafe which is popular not just with theatre-goers but also with locals. The food is freshly prepared at the bakers, Konditor and Cook, located around the corner from the cafe. Delicious croissants and pastries, tantalising breakfasts, and so on.

LEITH'S AT THE DESIGN MUSEUM
Shad Thames, SE1
Tel: 0171 357 8992
Situated next to the design shop at the museum, this spacious cafe looks out over the river and in summer benefits from a sun terrace. Delicious light lunches and flavoured coffees make a great break.

ANTIQUE SHOPS, DEALERS AND MARKETS

BERMONDSEY (NEW CALEDONIAN) MARKET
Bermondsey Square, SE1

Portobello's main rival, Bermondsey Market convenes on Friday's between 5 a.m. and 2 p.m. with a mixture of outdoor and indoor stalls.

BOROUGH MARKET
Southwark
Mainly a fruit and vegetable market, Borough Market brings a welcome splash of colour to this area which has often been used as a film location.

MUSEUMS

DESIGN MUSEUM
Shad Thames, SE1
Tel: 0171 357 8992
The Design Museum houses two galleries and a lecture theatre and has exhibitions of classic design from around the world. There is also a design shop.

BRAMAH TEA AND COFFEE MUSEUM
The Clove Building
Maguire Street
Butler's Wharf, SE1
Tel: 0171 378 0222
In the heart of the old tea and coffee trade at Butler's Wharf this

museum was established by Edward Bramah in 1992. It is the world's only complete collection devoted to the history of tea and coffee-making. There is also a cafe where both beverages can be sampled.

THE HAYWARD GALLERY
South Bank, SE1
Tel: 0171 928 3144
A series of temporary exhibitions.

MUSEUM OF GARDEN HISTORY
Tradescant Trust
St Mary-at-Lambeth
Lambeth Palace Road, SE1
Tel: 0171 261 1891
A permanent exhibition which explores garden history.

MUSEUM OF THE MOVING IMAGE
South Bank, SE1
Tel: 0171 401 2636
A museum which gives an intriguing insight into the history of cinema and television. An ideal place for children, it includes multimedia and interactive displays and is well documented.

Dulwich

RESTAURANTS

BELAIR HOUSE
Gallery Road
Dulwich Village, SE21
Tel: 0181 299 9788
This airy restaurant, in a listed Georgian house near the Dulwich Picture Gallery, also has a bar which serves breakfast. Good fish

dishes and a modern British cuisine.

ATTRACTIONS

DULWICH PICTURE GALLERY
College Road, SE21
Tel: 0181 693 5254
Britain's oldest picture gallery, the building

was designed in 1811 by Sir John Soane to contain not only a gallery but also a mausoleum for the benefactors, as well as new almshouses.
The exhibition features eighteenth-century English portraits, Dutch and Flemish paintings, and seventeenth century French, Spanish and

Italian paintings in the Grand Style.

THE HORNIMAN MUSEUM & GARDENS
100 London Road
Forest Hill, SE23
Tel: 0181 699 1872
The gardens of this unexpected museum were originally part of Frederick Horn-

iman's Surrey Mount home and are laid out over one of the highest hills in London, affording spectacular views back over the City. The museum itself is a treasure trove of adventure, for children in particular, with a Living Waters Aquarium and a wonderful Natural History Collection.

Greenwich

MUSEUMS

NATIONAL MARITIME MUSEUM
Romney Road, SE10
Tel: 0181 858 4422
The Old Royal Observatory and the Queen's House are included in the admission fee of this museum dedicated to British Naval history.

RESTAURANTS

TAI WAN MEIN (NOODLE HOUSE)
49 Greenwich Church Street, SE10
Tel.: 0181 858 1668
Obligatory wooden benches and refectory tables create a minimalist, healthy background for a fresh, Japanese-inspired cuisine. Raw fruit and vegetable juice a popular starter.

SPREAD EAGLE
1-2 Stockwell Street, SE10
Tel.: 0181 853 2333
A former coaching inn and erstwhile haunt of famous actors, the dining room serves French cuisine in a cosy, atmosphere-laden setting while the entrance hall is filled with the memorabilia of the inn's past.

GODDARD'S YE OLD PIE HOUSE
45 Greenwich Church Street SE10
Newspaper clippings recounting the history of Greenwich line the walls of this popular restaurant. Taking advantage of the hordes of visitors who come to Greenwich during the summer, tourists and locals alike can sample genuine freshly baked pies and mash, served with thick brown gravy.

PUBS

NORTH POLE
131 Greenwich High Road, SE10
Tel.: 0181 853 3020
One of the new style pubs with a good restaurant, the recently renovated North Pole now boasts a purple ground floor with luxurious upholstered sofas in the corners. The restaurant is located upstairs in a pared-down atmosphere of rough brick walls and wooden tables, where light, fashionable Mediterranean food is served.

ASHBURNHAM ARMS
25 Ashburnham Grove, SE10
Tel.: 0181 692 2007
Situated on a quiet residential street, this unpretentious pub is a local favourite offering a good selection of lagers and ales.

CUTTY SARK
Ballast Quay
off Lassell Street
SE10
Tel.: 0181 858 3146
Located right on the Thames about half a mile downriver past the boat from which it takes its name, there has been a pub on this site since 1695. The current building is only 200 years old, decorated in a nautical style, and has a deserved reputation for its beer as well as its food.

Richmond and West of London

HOTELS

PETERSHAM
Nightingale Lane,
TW10 6UZ
Tel: 0181 940 7471
A charming fifty-seven room hotel near Richmond Park with a good restaurant.

ATTRACTIONS

CHISWICK HOUSE
Burlington Lane, W4
Tel: 0181 995 0508
This Palladian villa was designed by Lord Burlington in 1729 and created enormous excitement when it was finished. Londoners planned day trips out to visit the building and Lord Burlington even opened it to the public in the afternoons and charged an admission fee! (see page 46).

HAM HOUSE
Ham, Richmond, TW10 7RS
Tel: 0181 940 1950
A seventeenth-century manor house and garden—now managed by the National Trust—furnished with original pieces and provides a fascinating insight into the life of the time (see pages 56, 57, and 184).

HAMPTON COURT PALACE
Surrey, KT8 9U
Tel: 0181 781 9500
Former royal residence to many early British monarchs, Hampton Court is open to the public and has wonderful gardens which run along the Thames.

HOGARTH'S HOUSE
Hogarth Lane
Great West Road, W4
Tel: 0181 994 6757
Former home of William Hogarth, well-known for his drawings and truisms of eighteenth-century London. It is located close to Chiswick House.

OSTERLEY PARK
Isleworth
Middlesex, TW7 4RB
Tel: 0181 568 3164
Restored and remodelled by Robert Adam in 1761, Osterley Park is one of the great showpieces of this great master's work. Visitors marvel at the beautiful neo-classical rooms and furniture (see pages 185–187).

PITSHANGER MANOR MUSEUM
Mattock Lane
Ealing, W5
Tel: 0181 567 1227
Pitshanger Manor was designed by Sir John Soane as his country villa and was opened to the public in 1987, 150 years after his death. Bereft of much of its furniture, which has been moved to the Soane Museum in Lincoln's Inn Fields, Pitshanger Manor remains the beautiful shell of an architect's dream (see page 184).

THE ROYAL BOTANICAL GARDENS AT KEW
Tel: 0181 332 5000
Secluded and private behind a high brick wall, Kew Gardens is not only a place of beauty and variety but also a source of botanical information renowned throughout the world (see page 63).

SYON PARK
Brentford
Tel: 0181 560 0881
Seat of the Duke of Northumberland and remodelled by Robert Adam in 1762, Syon House is a beautiful place to tour. The park was landscaped by Capability Brown and the grounds include a garden centre and a trout fishery.

SPECIALIST SHOPS

THE DINING ROOM SHOP
62–64 White Hart Lane
Barnes, SW13
Tel: 0181 878 1020
A unique shop which specialises in everything to do with the dining room, both antique and new.

BIBLIOGRAPHY

Of particular help in the research of this book:

• *David Gentleman's London*, Trafalgar Square, 1999
• *John Hillaby's London*, Constable, 1987
• Brace & Frankl, *London Parks & Gardens*, Pevensey Press, 1986
• John Bignell, *Chelsea seen from 1860 to 1980: a collection of photographs old and new*
• Mary Cathcart Borer, *Hampstead & Highgate*, W.H. Allen, 1976
• Nathan Cole, *Royal Parks & Gardens of London*, 1877
• Barbara Denny, *Notting Hill and Holland Park Past: A Visual History*, Historical Publications, 1993
• Joe Friedman, *Inside London: Discovering London's Period Interiors*, Phaidon, 1997
• Charles Harris, *Islington*, H. Hamilton Press, 1974
• Humphries & Taylor, *The Making of Modern London 1945-85*, Sidgwick & Jackson, 1986
• Nerina Shute, *London Villages*, St Martins Press, 1977
• Annabel Walker and Peter Jacks, *Kensington & Chelsea: A Social and Architectural History*
• Ben Weinreb and Christopher Hibbert (eds.), *The London Encyclopaedia*, Macmillan, 1983

Other books currently available on London:

Guides

• *AA All in One Guide - London*, AA Publishing, 1998
• *AA Explorer - London*, AA Publishing, 1998
• *Berlitz Travellers London*, Alan Tucker, ed., 1994
• *Blue Guide London*, Ylva French, W.W. Norton & Company, 1998
• *Everyman City Guides - London*, Campbell Publishing, 1998
• *Eye Witness Travel Guides - London*, DK Publishing, 1998
• *Fodor's Up Close - London*, Fodor's Travel, 1998
• *Fodor's London Companion*, Louise Nicholson, Fodor, 1987 (ed. 1993)
• *Frommer's 1999 Portable London*, Arthur Frommer, Darwin Porter, Danforth Prince, Frommer, 1999
• *Frommer's Irreverent Guide: London*, London, 1998
• *A Guide to the Architecture of London*, Edward Jones and Christopher Woodward, Van Nostrand Reinhold, 1983
• *Harden's London for Free*, Harden's Guides, 1998
• *Harden's London Restaurants 1998*, Richard Harden, Peter Harden, Harden, 1998
• *The House & Garden Book of Essential Addresses*, Nicolette Le Pelley and Cheryl Knorr, Design Line, 1997
• *Insight Guide London*, Apa Productions, 1998
• *Let's Go London*, Macmillan, 1999
• *The London Market Guide*, Philip Harris, Cadogan, 1999
• *London - The Rough Guide*, Rob Humphreys, 1998
• *London Pub & Bar Guide*, Edward Sullivan, Simon & Schuster, 1999

• *London for Less: The Total Guidebook*, Ben West, Metropolis International, 1997
• *London's Good Coffee Shops*, Shaun Beary, 1997
• *London, England - A day-tripper's travelogue from the coolest city in the world*, Derek Hammond, Mainstream Publishing, Edinburgh, 1998
• *Lonely Planet - London*, 1998
Museums & Galleries of London, Abigail Willis, Metro Publications, 1998
• *The Mysteries of London*, G.W.M. Reynolds, Keele University Press, 1996
• *The Oxford Book of London*, Paul Bailey (Editor), Larry Bailey, Oxford University Press, 1997
• *Time Out Guide - London*, Penguin, 1998
• *Time Out Guide Pubs & Bars 1998*
• *Village London: A Guide to London's Neighbourhoods*, Andrew Duncan, Passport Books, 1997
• *Walking London: Thirty Original Walks In and Around London*, Andrew Duncan, NTC Publishing Group, 1999
• *Walking London's Parks and Gardens*, Geoffrey Young, Passport Books, 1998

Literature

• Peter Ackroyd, *Blake*, Minerva Press, 1996
• Peter Ackroyd, *Hawksmoor*, Penguin, 1993
• Peter Ackroyd, *The House of Dr. Dee*, Penguin, 1994
• Julian Barnes, *Letters from London*, Picador, 1995
• J.M. Barrie, *Peter Pan*, Hodder, 1995

• Oliver Benn and Andrew Eames, *Benn's London*, Bouverie House, 1998
• James Boswell, *The Life of Samuel Johnson*, Penguin, 1979
• Ted Bruning, *Historic Pubs of London*, Prion Books, 1998
• Kellow Chesney, *The Victorian Underworld*, Penguin, 1991
• Hugh D. Clout (ed.), *The Times London History Atlas*, 1997, Times Books
• Daniel Defoe, *A Journal of the Plague Year*, Penguin, 1970
• Daniel Farson, *Never a Normal Man*, Harper Collins, 1998
• Warren Grynberg, *The Square Mile: City of London in Historic Postcards*, Windrush, 1995
• Jason Hawkes, *London Landmarks from the Air*, Ebury Press, 1996
• Alethea Hayter, *A Sultry Month: Scenes of London Literary Life in 1846*, R. Clark, 1992
• Christopher Hibbert, *London, The Biography of a City*, Penguin, 1969 (ed. 1977)
• Christopher Hibbert, *The Personal History of Samuel Johnson*, Pimlico, 1998
• Molly Hughes, *A London Family 1870-1900*, Oxford University Press, 1991
• Jonathan Kiek, *Everybody's Historic London*, Quiller, 1997
• David Kynaston, *The City of London Volume I - A World of Its Own 1815-1890*, Pimlico, 1995
• David Kynaston, *The City*

of London Volume II - Golden Years 1890-1914, Chatto & Windus, 1995
• Ford Madox Ford, *The Soul of London*, Everyman, 1995
• Henry Mayhew, *London Labour and the London Poor*, Penguin Classics, 1985
• Henrietta Moraes, *Henrietta*, Penguin, 1995
• Rowan More & Sampson Lloyd, *Panoramas of London*, Phoenix, 1997
• Louise Nicholson, *London*, Frances Lincoln, 1998
• David Paterson, *London: City on a River*, Peak Publishing, 1998
• Samuel Pepys (Robert Latham, ed.), *The Shorter Pepys*, Penguin Classics, 1993
• Nikolaus Pevsner, *London*, Penguin, 1991
• Liza Picard, *Restoration London*, Weidenfeld & Nicolson, 1997
• Roy Porter, *London, A Social History*, Penguin, 1994
• Stephen Porter, *The Great Fire of London*, Sutton Publishing, 1998
• John Russell, *London*, Thames & Hudson, 1996
• Denise Silvester-Carr, *London: A City Revealed*, AA Publishing, 1997
• Iain Sinclair, *Lights out for the Territory*, Granta Books, 1997
• John Stow, *A Survey of London*, orig. 1598, Sutton Publishing, 1994 (reprinted 1997)
• A.N. Wilson (ed.), *The Faber Book of London*, Faber & Faber, 1994
• Derek Wilson, *The Tower of London, A Thousand Years*, Allison & Busby, 1998

ACKNOWLEDGEMENTS

Our thanks to the following people for their generosity and support in helping to put this book together:

Peter Ackroyd, Claudio Silvestrin, Martin Lane, Lord Snowdon, George Carter, Olga Polizzi, Deborah James, Oriel Harwood, Dennis Severs, Angela Enthoven, Diane Berger, Keith Skeel, Christopher Gibbs, Min Hogg, Christophe Gollut, Hugo Vickers, Frances Partridge, Joan Hecktermann, Gul Coskun, Clare Lloyd, Sir Terence Conran, Vicky Davis, Simon Willis, Paul and Sue Vaight, Timothy Everest, Stephen Calloway, François Gilles, Trudy Ballard, Lady Weinberg, John Morgan and especially to Lawrence Kane and Lolita Howes. A thank-you also to our editor, Ghislaine Bavoillot and her assistant Maud Bioret for their direction and enthusiasm.

INDEX

UNIVERSITY OF WOLVERHAMPTON LEARNING RESOURCES